# Hey, Andrew! Teach Me Some Greek!

## A BIBLICAL GREEK WORKTEXT

### LEVEL 1
ANSWER KEY

BY KAREN MOHS

Dear Parent/Teacher:

This answer key is designed to assist you in teaching Greek Workbook Level One.

Please note the "More Practice" pages (directly following the introduction of each new letter or word). These pages are beneficial in firmly planting the new item into the student's memory. It is best if they are completed.

Occasionally, however, too much repetition can cool a student's enthusiasm. For some, half a page of practice will be adequate. You are the best judge of your student's needs and abilities.

Daily flashcard practice is essential. Please do not neglect this effective learning tool. The letters for flashcard use are located at the end of the workbook.

A glossary at the end of the workbook defines Greek words used in the letter recognition exercises.

In addition to this answer key, quizzes/exams and flashcards on a ring are available. The audio pronunciation CD or cassette tape includes Greek letters, vocabulary, "The Greek Alphabet Song," and a reading of *The Reader*.

Most importantly, make this an enjoyable learning experience and a happy memory for both you and your student.

References:
    *New Testament Greek For Beginners* by J. Gresham Machen
    *Essentials of New Testament Greek* by Ray Summers
    *A Short Syntax of New Testament Greek* by H.P.V. Nunn
    *Moods and Tenses of New Testament Greek* by Earnest De Witt Burton
    *A Manual Grammar of the Greek New Testament* by Dana and Mantey
    *Exhaustive Concordance of the Bible* by James Strong

Copyright © 1994 by Karen Mohs
All rights reserved. No part of this publication may be reproduced without prior permission of the author.

ISBN-13: 978-1-931842-02-0
ISBN-10: 1-931842-02-7

Greek 'n' Stuff
P.O. Box 882
Moline, IL 61266-0882
www.greeknstuff.com

Revised 1/05

# SCHEDULE OF LESSONS
## (PROPOSAL FOR LEVEL ONE)

In overview, the *Hey, Andrew! Teach Me Some Greek!* workbooks are designed such that the student ideally completes one page per day (and practices his or her flashcards each day as well). (It should be noted that older students often complete more than one page per day when they are working in the early levels.) The workbooks were not designed within a framework of "lessons." Many parents have told us they appreciate this approach. It is easy to follow, without need of additional parent/teacher preparation and scheduling.

However, some parents/teachers prefer the "lesson" approach. Please be aware that this "Schedule of Lessons" is an artificial grid placed over a series not written with this grid in mind. The assigned pages are arbitrary and should be modified so the student can progress through the workbooks at a pace suitable to his or her age/skill level.

A note about our methodology:
    This series begins gently and advances gradually, providing plenty of reinforcement through a wide variety of workbook activities and translation exercises. By introducing new concepts slowly, *Hey, Andrew! Teach Me Some Greek!* avoids the pitfall common to many foreign language courses whereby the student suddenly faces a steep learning curve, becomes frustrated, fails to internalize the language, and develops an aversion to foreign language study in general. The overwhelming response from those using *Hey, Andrew! Teach Me Some Greek!* can be summed up by the words we hear so often: "This is my student's favorite subject."

### Lesson 1
    Pages 1-4 - Alphabet letter alpha, alphabet practice

> *Teacher tip:*
>     For more information on the alphabet, see Lesson 1 of *New Testament Greek for Beginners* by J. Gresham Machen or pages 7-12 of *Basics of Biblical Greek* by William D. Mounce.

### Lesson 2
    Pages 5-8 - Alphabet letter beta, alphabet practice

### Lesson 3
    Pages 9-12 - Alphabet letter gamma, alphabet practice

### Lesson 4
    Pages 13-16 - Alphabet letter delta, alphabet practice

**Lesson 5**
    Pages 17-20 - Alphabet letter epsilon, alphabet practice

**Lesson 6**
    Pages 21-24 - Alphabet letter zeta, alphabet practice

**Lesson 7**
    Pages 25-28 - Alphabet letter eta, alphabet practice

```
***********
QUIZ #1 (optional)
***********
```

**Lesson 8**
    Pages 29-32 - Alphabet letter theta, alphabet practice

**Lesson 9**
    Pages 33-36 - Alphabet letter iota, alphabet practice

**Lesson 10**
    Pages 37-40 - Alphabet letter kappa, alphabet practice

**Lesson 11**
    Pages 41-44 - Alphabet letter lambda, alphabet practice

**Lesson 12**
    Pages 45-48 - Alphabet letter mu, alphabet practice

**Lesson 13**
    Pages 49-52 - Alphabet letter nu, alphabet practice

**Lesson 14**
    Pages 53-56 - Alphabet letter xi, alphabet practice

```
***********
QUIZ #2 (optional)
***********
```

```
*****************
MIDTERM EXAM (optional)
*****************
```

**Lesson 15**
    Pages 57-60 - Alphabet letter omicron, alphabet practice

**Lesson 16**
    Pages 61-64 - Alphabet letter pi, alphabet practice

**Lesson 17**
    Pages 65-68 - Alphabet letter rho, alphabet practice

**Lesson 18**
    Pages 69-72 - Alphabet letter sigma, alphabet practice

**Lesson 19**
    Pages 73-76 - Alphabet letter tau, alphabet practice

**Lesson 20**
    Pages 77-80 - Alphabet letter upsilon, alphabet practice

    \*\*\*\*\*\*\*\*\*\*\*
    QUIZ #3 (optional)
    \*\*\*\*\*\*\*\*\*\*\*

**Lesson 21**
    Pages 81-84 - Alphabet letter phi, alphabet practice

**Lesson 22**
    Pages 85-88 - Alphabet letter chi, alphabet practice

**Lesson 23**
    Pages 89-92 - Alphabet letter psi, alphabet practice

**Lesson 24**
    Pages 93-96 - Alphabet letter omega, alphabet practice

    \*\*\*\*\*\*\*\*\*\*\*
    QUIZ #4 (optional)
    \*\*\*\*\*\*\*\*\*\*\*

**Lesson 25**
    Pages 97-98 - Greek word κύριος, vocabulary practice

> *English derivatives:*
>     κύριος (Kyrie, church, kirk)

**Lesson 26**
    Pages 99-102 - Greek word ἐμοὶ, vocabulary practice

**Lesson 27**
    Pages 103-106 - Greek word βοηθός, vocabulary practice

**Lesson 28**
    Pages 107 - Greek sentence

```
***********
QUIZ #5 (optional)
***********

***************
FINAL EXAM (optional)
***************
```

**Appendix**

| | |
|---|---|
| Greek - English Glossary | 109 |
| Greek Alphabet | 111 |
| Vowels and Diphthongs | 111 |
| Flashcard Tips | 112 |

Lesson 1

# ALPHA

(Put your pencil here and trace the letter.)

Write the letter *alpha* across each line.
As you write it, say "**al**-fa."

a    a    a    a    a

a    a    a    a    a

Greek Workbook - Level 1
Copyright © 1994 by Karen Mohs

# More Practice with ALPHA

Alpha sounds like **a** in *father*.

α α α α α

α α α α α

α α α α α

α α α α α

α α α α α

α α α α α

α α α α α

Greek Workbook - Level 1
Copyright © 1994 by Karen Mohs

# REMEMBER!
## Alpha sounds like **a** in *father*.

Circle the words that have the alpha sound.

(cot)           great

(lark)          (palm)

math            (guard)

fan             rat

(sonic)         tame

(watch)         day

him             (jar)

# LET'S PRACTICE

Make little alphas in this giant alpha.

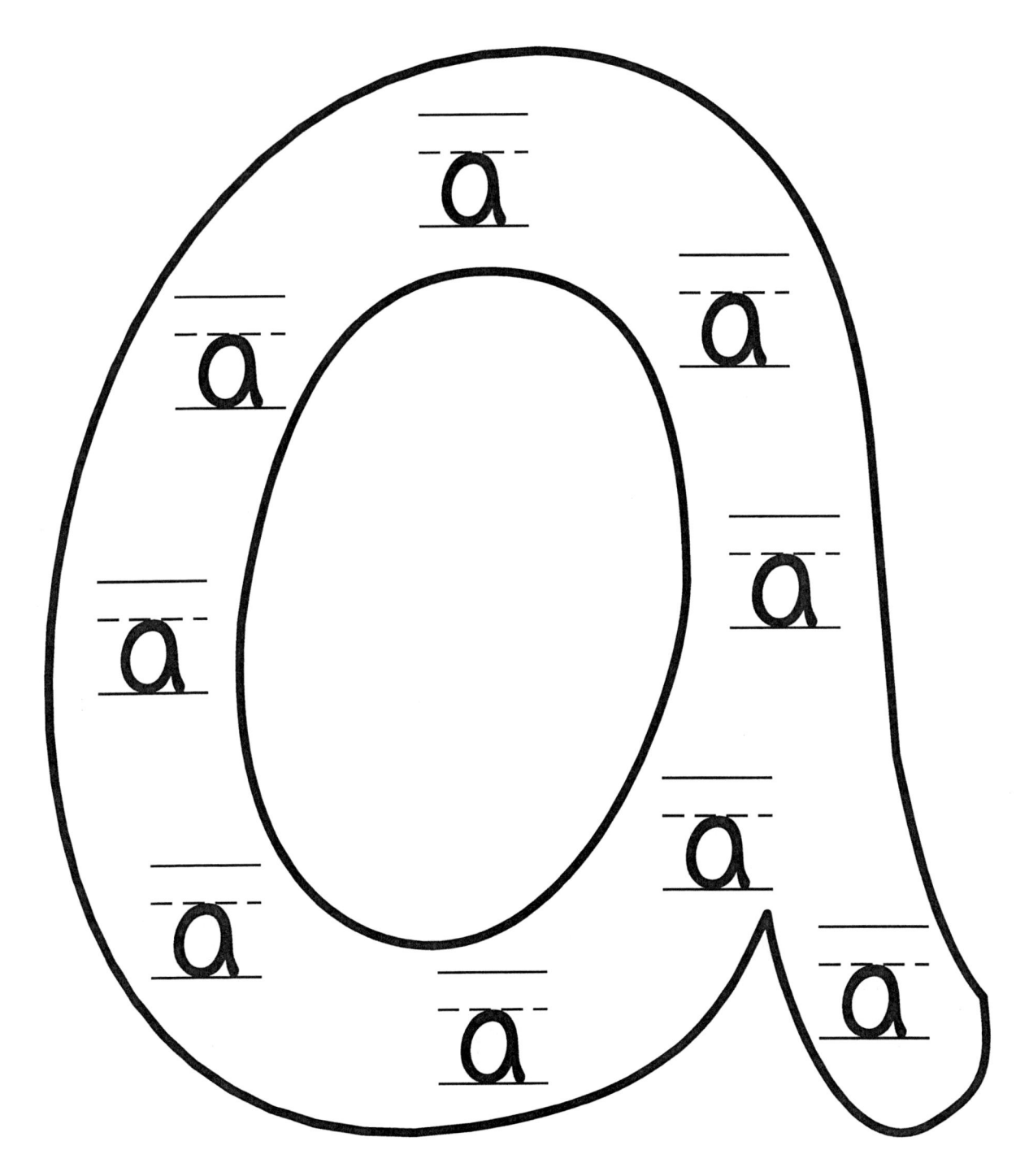

Lesson 2

# BETA

Write the letter *beta* across each line.
As you write it, say "**bay**-ta."

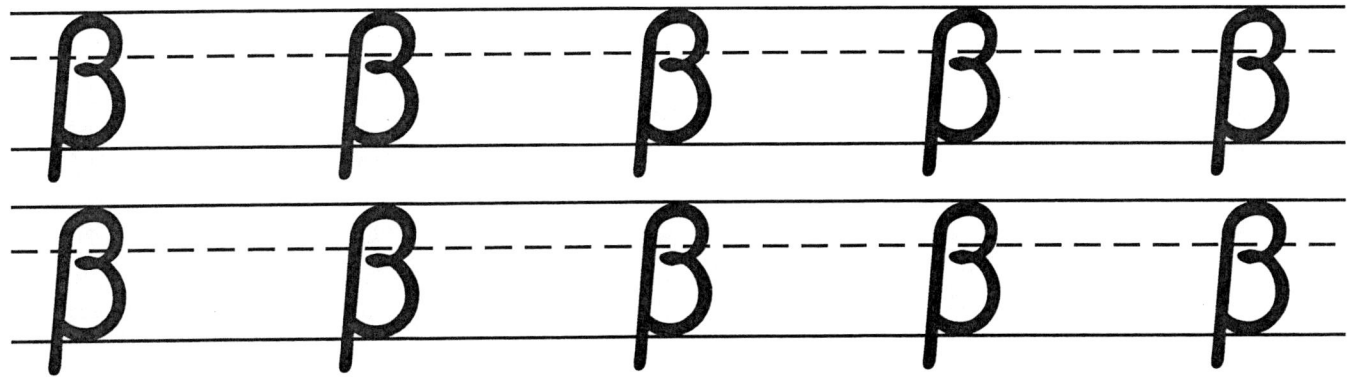

β   β   β   β   β

β   β   β   β   β

# More Practice with BETA

Beta sounds like **b** in *bat*.

β  β  β  β  β

β  β  β  β  β

β  β  β  β  β

β  β  β  β  β

β  β  β  β  β

β  β  β  β  β

β  β  β  β  β

# LET'S PRACTICE

Draw lines from the words that have the beta sound to the big beta in the middle of the page.

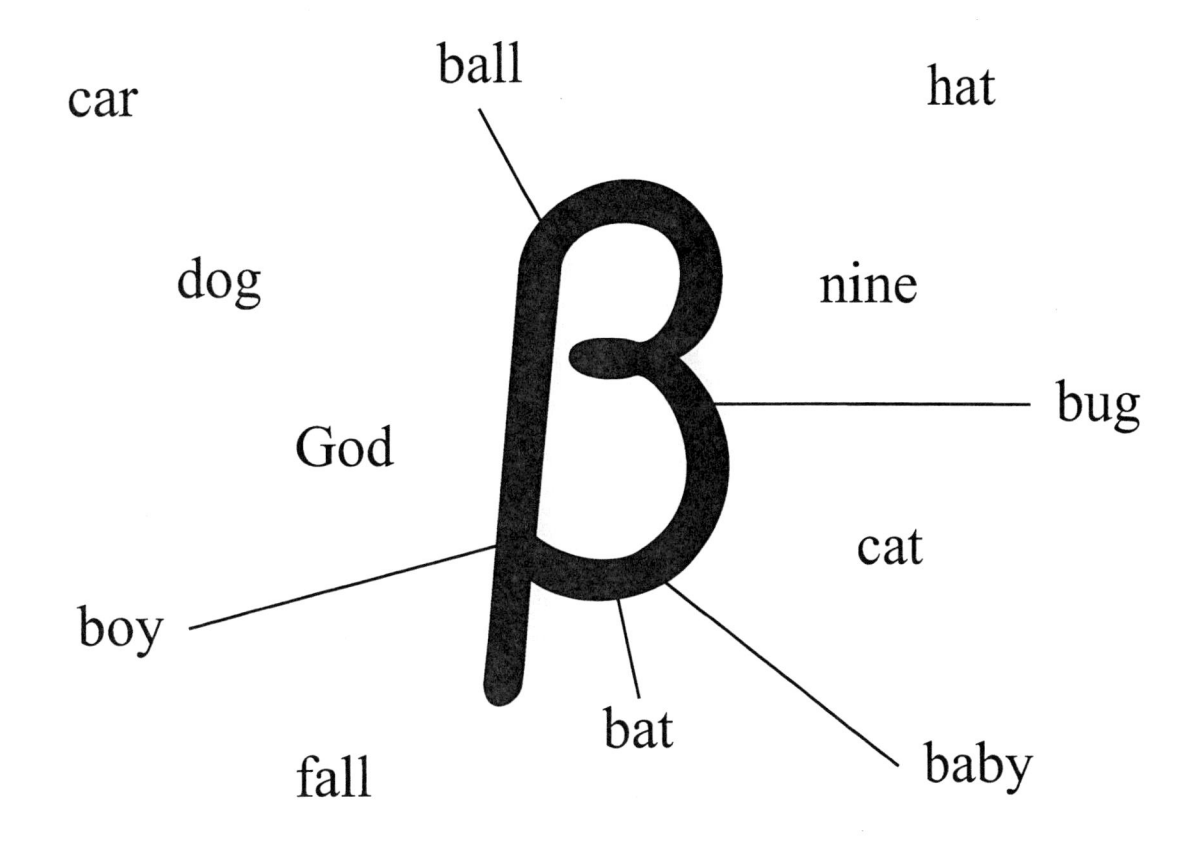

ball — β
car
hat
dog
nine
bug — β
God
cat
boy — β
bat
baby — β
fall

---

You now know the first two letters of the Greek alphabet. Start your flashcard deck with these letters and practice them every day.
(See back of workbook for flashcards.)
☐ I practiced my flashcards today.

# LET'S PRACTICE

Draw lines from the Greek letters to their names.

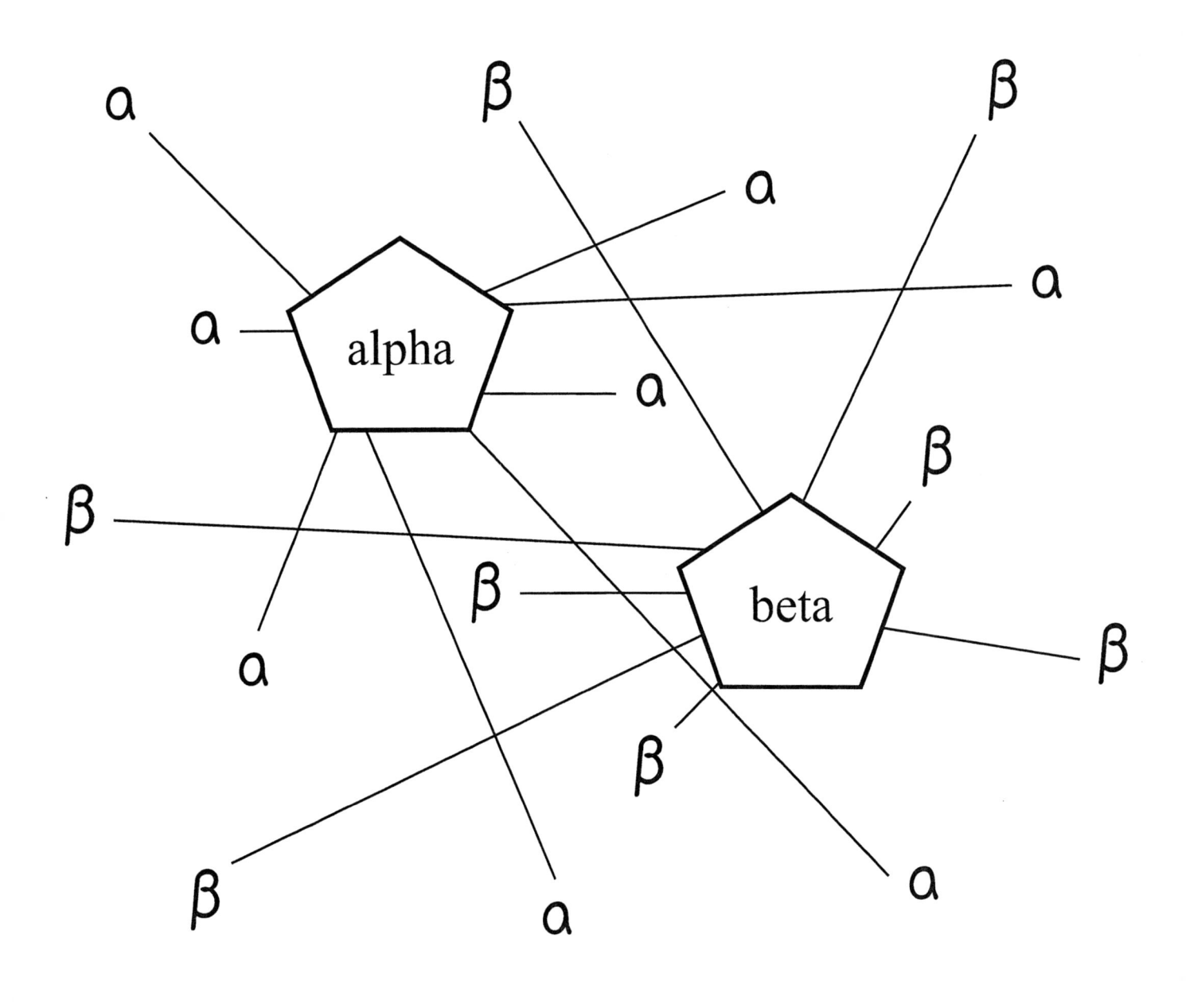

☐ I practiced my flashcards today.

Lesson 3

# GAMMA

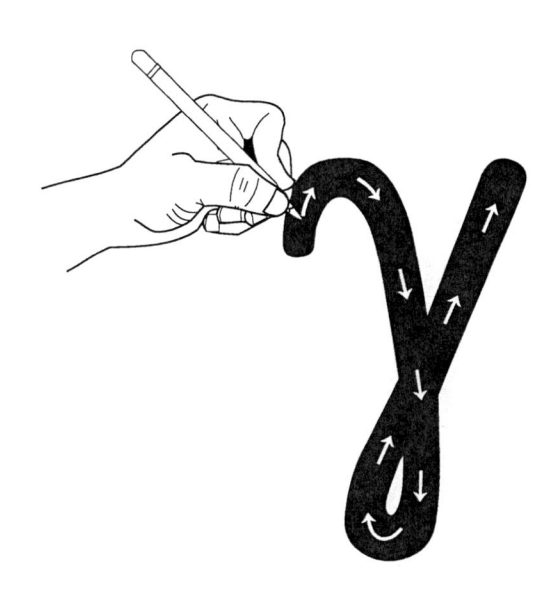

Write the letter *gamma* across each line.
As you write it, say "**gam**-ma."

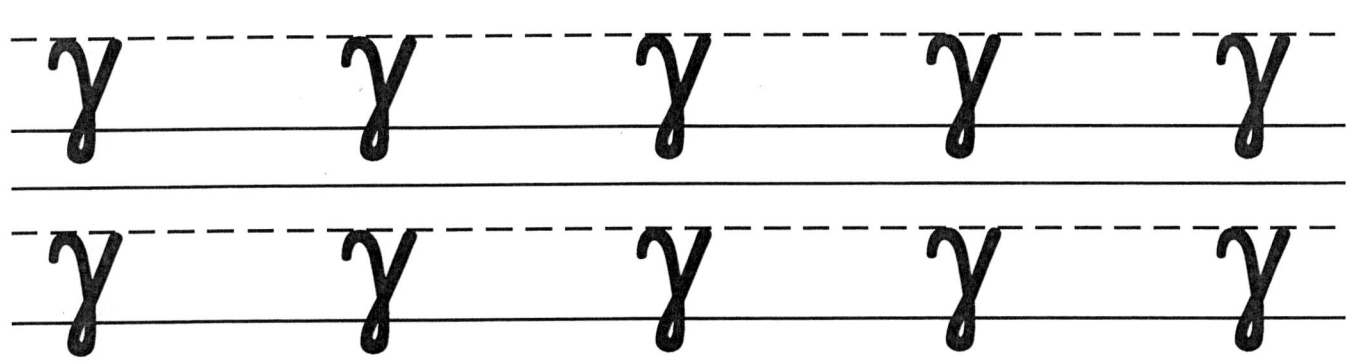

γ  γ  γ  γ  γ

γ  γ  γ  γ  γ

Greek Workbook - Level 1
Copyright © 1994 by Karen Mohs

9

# More Practice with GAMMA

Gamma sounds like **g** in *God*.

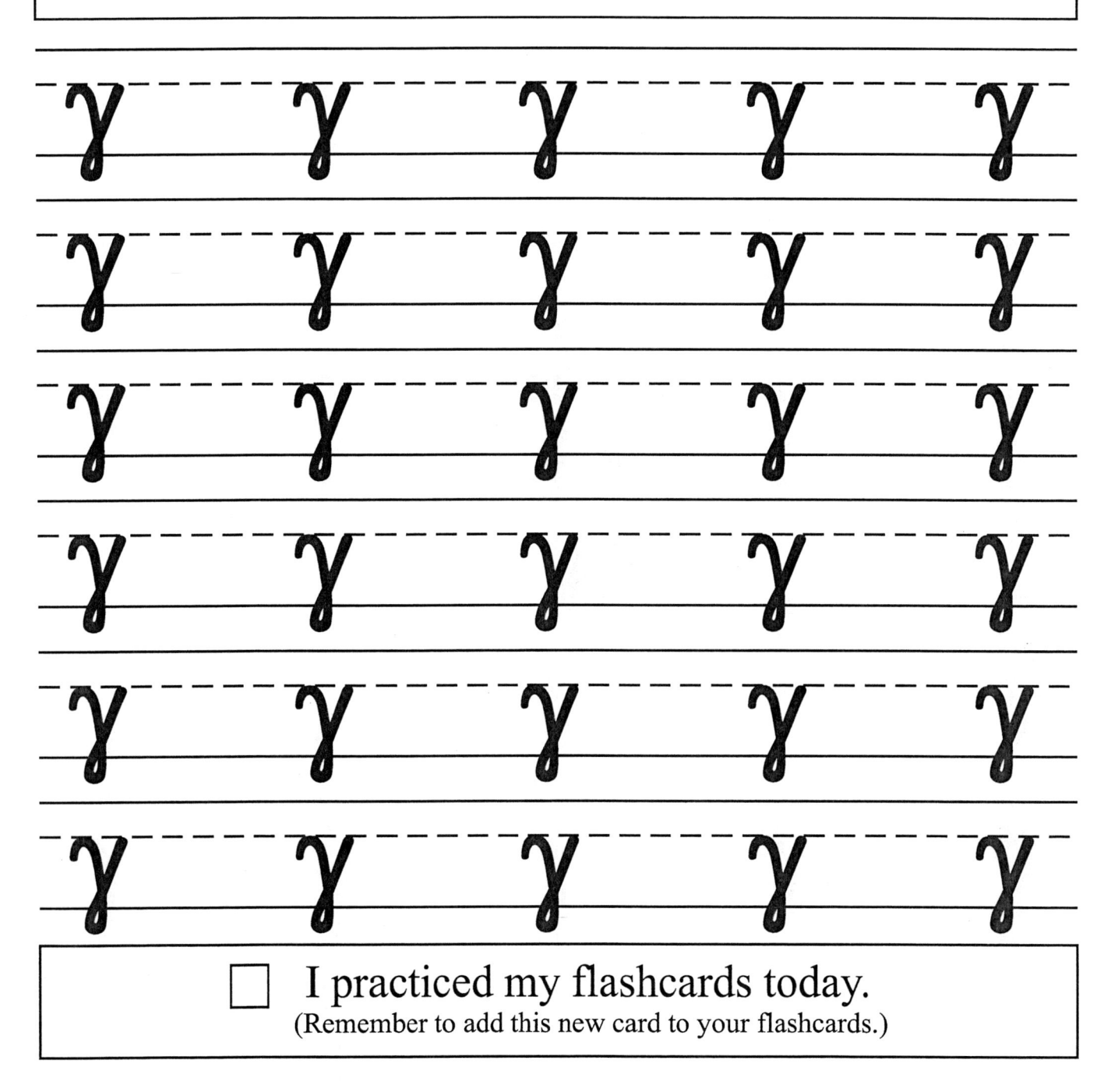

γ  γ  γ  γ  γ

γ  γ  γ  γ  γ

γ  γ  γ  γ  γ

γ  γ  γ  γ  γ

γ  γ  γ  γ  γ

γ  γ  γ  γ  γ

☐ I practiced my flashcards today.
(Remember to add this new card to your flashcards.)

# LET'S PRACTICE

Write three letters of the Greek alphabet in order.

α  β  γ

Draw lines from the Greek letters to their names.

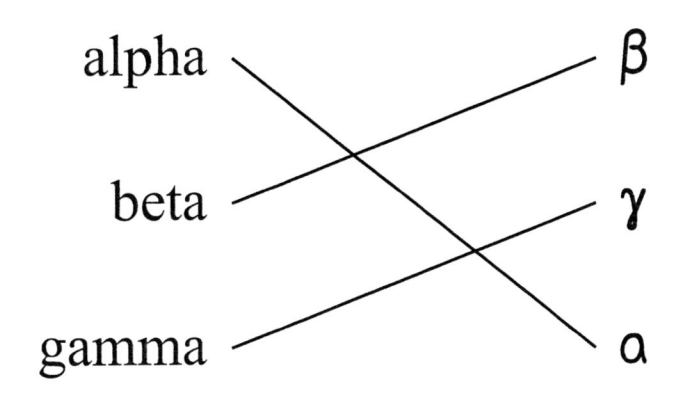

alpha — β
beta — γ
gamma — α

Circle the Greek letters.

g  z  (β)  j
 (α)      m
  (γ)
d           c

☐ I practiced my flashcards today.

# LET'S PRACTICE

WHAT'S MY SOUND? Draw lines from the Greek letters to the words that have their sounds.

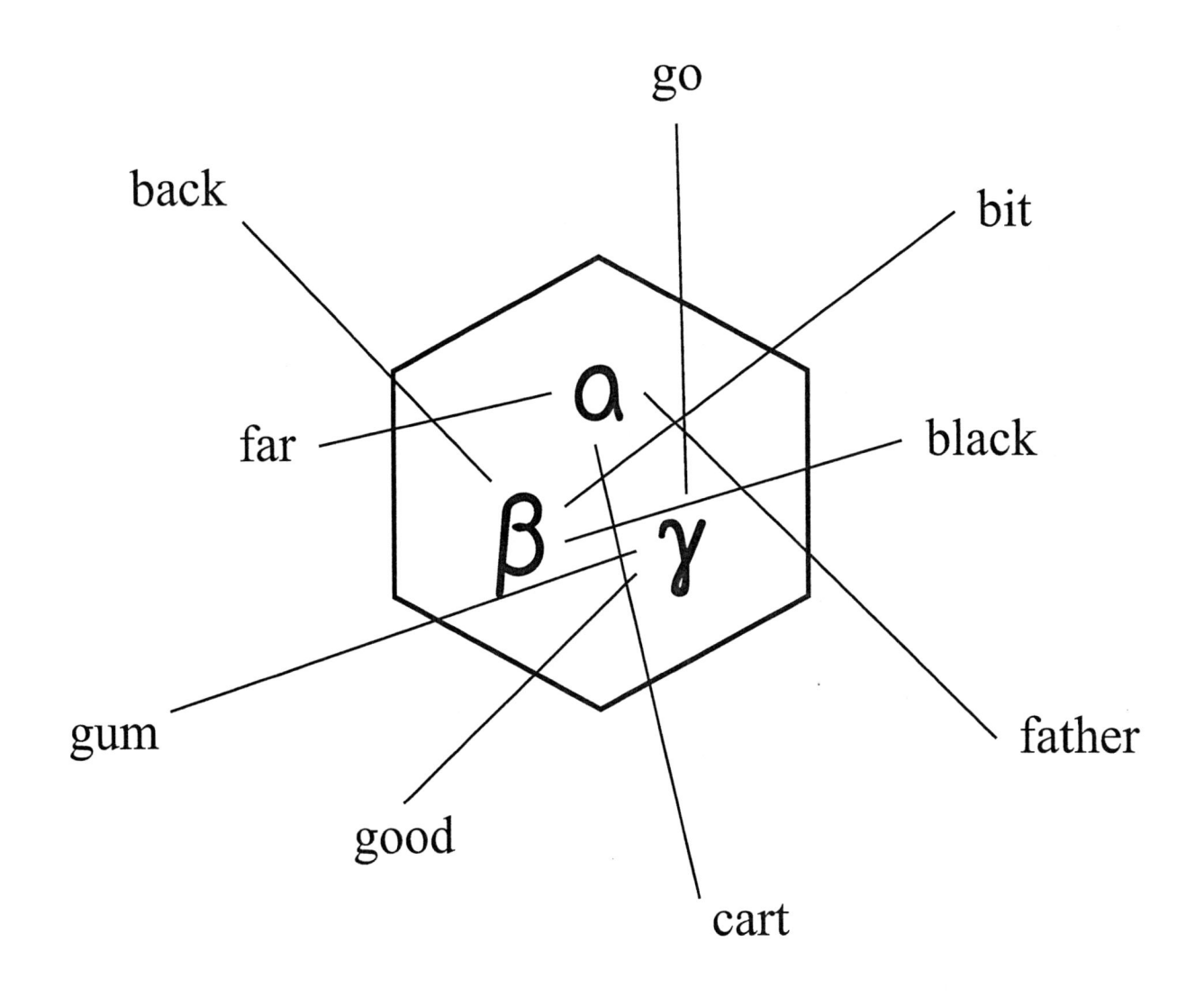

- go
- back
- bit
- far
- black
- α
- β
- γ
- gum
- father
- good
- cart

☐ I practiced my flashcards today.

Greek Workbook - Level 1
Copyright © 1994 by Karen Mohs

Lesson 4

# DELTA

Write the letter *delta* across each line.
As you write it, say "**del**-ta."

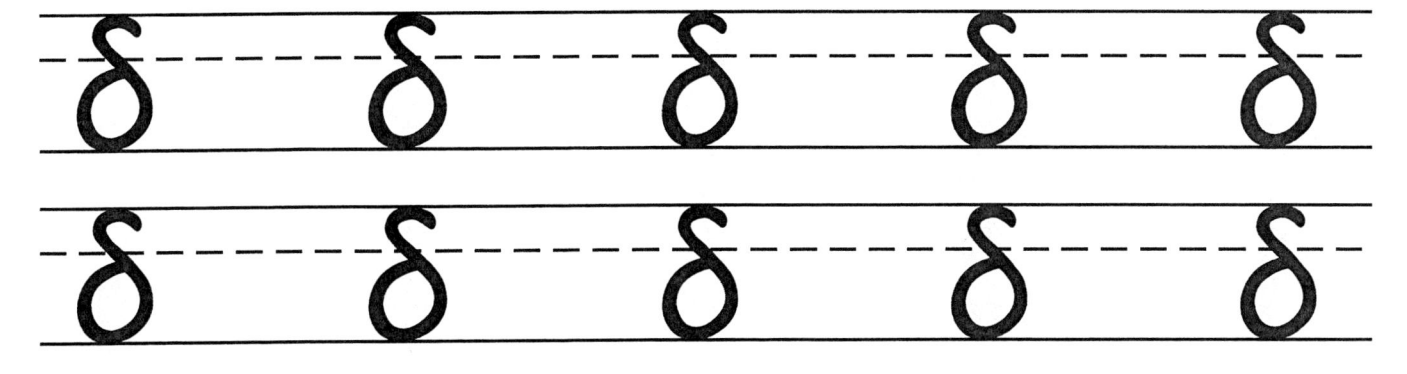

δ  δ  δ  δ  δ

δ  δ  δ  δ  δ

# More Practice with DELTA

Delta sounds like **d** in *dog*.

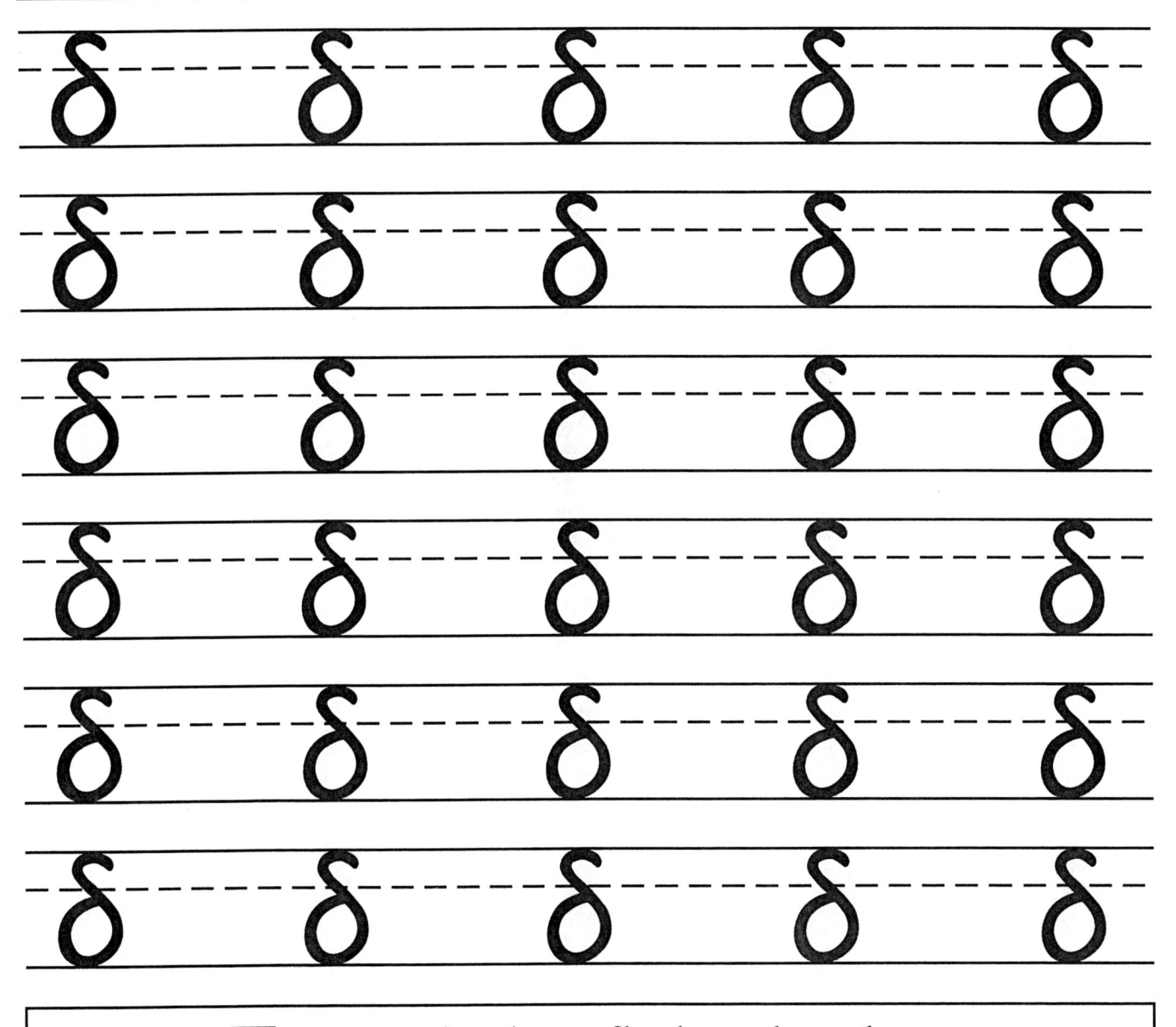

δ δ δ δ δ

δ δ δ δ δ

δ δ δ δ δ

δ δ δ δ δ

δ δ δ δ δ

δ δ δ δ δ

☐ I practiced my flashcards today.
(Remember to add this new card to your flashcards.)

# LET'S PRACTICE

Write four letters of the Greek alphabet in order.

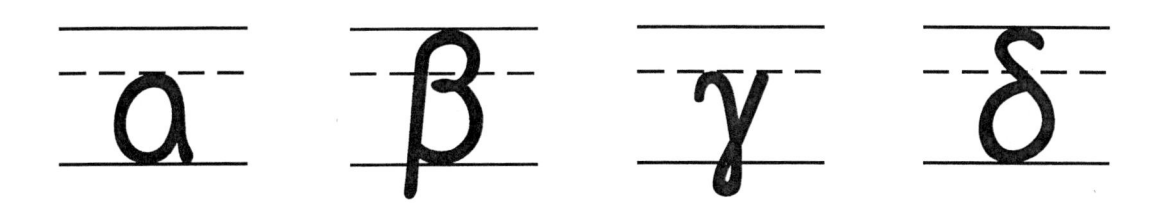

α   β   γ   δ

Write the names of the Greek letters.

α   alpha

β   beta

γ   gamma

δ   delta

Blacken the boxes containing the Greek letters. Then read the message.

| β | I | γ | β | L | O | V | E | α | γ | G | R | E | E | K | α |

☐   I practiced my flashcards today.

# LET'S PRACTICE

Draw lines from the Greek letters to their sounds.

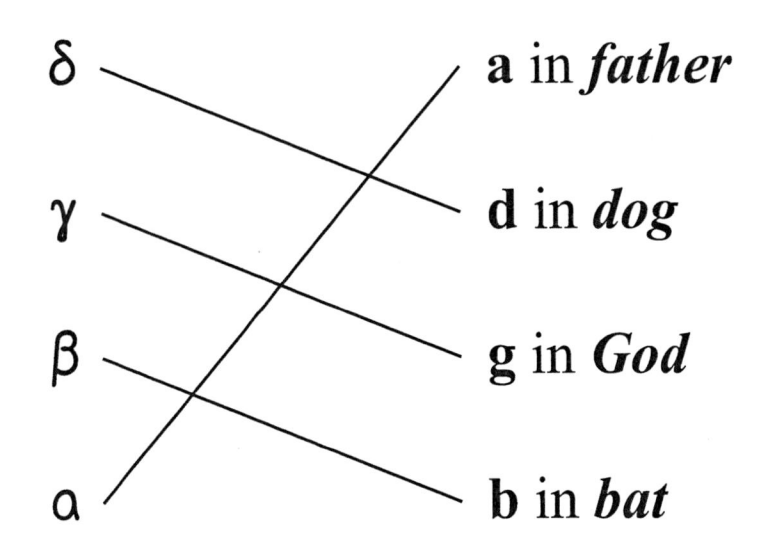

δ — a in *father*

γ — d in *dog*

β — g in *God*

α — b in *bat*

Fill in the missing parts of the Greek letters.

α     β     γ     δ

<u>  alpha  </u>    <u>  beta  </u>    <u>  gamma  </u>    <u>  delta  </u>

Now write their names on the lines.

☐ I practiced my flashcards today.

# EPSILON

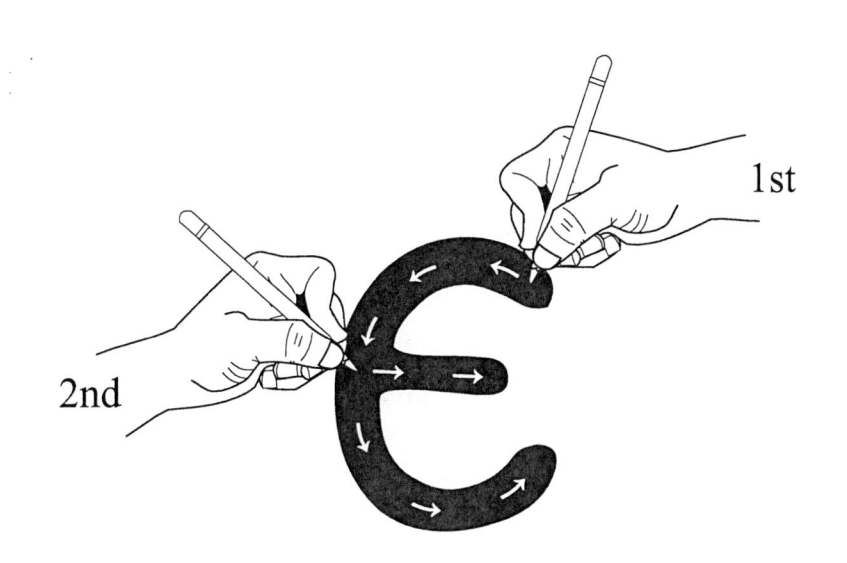

Write the letter *epsilon* across each line.
As you write it, say "**ep**-si-lon."

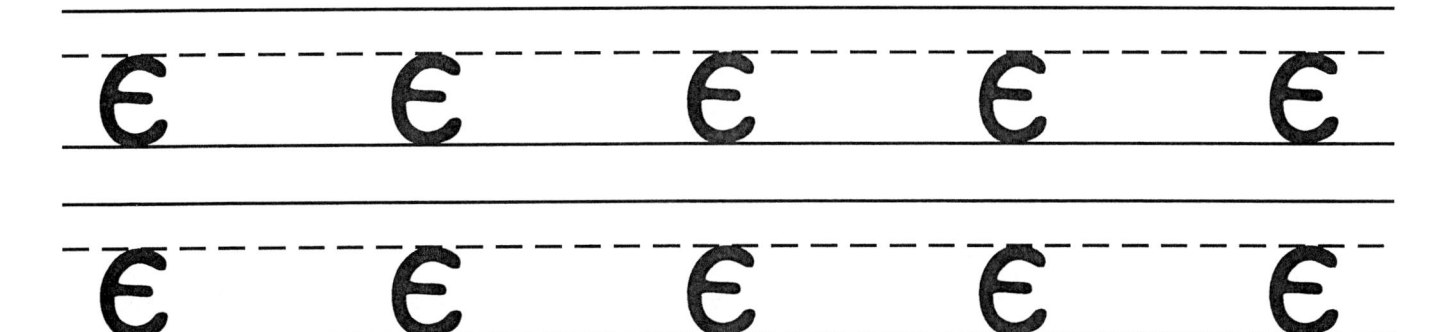

# More Practice with EPSILON

Epsilon sounds like **e** in *get*.

ε   ε   ε   ε   ε

ε   ε   ε   ε   ε

ε   ε   ε   ε   ε

ε   ε   ε   ε   ε

ε   ε   ε   ε   ε

ε   ε   ε   ε   ε

☐ I practiced my flashcards today.
(Remember to add this new card to your flashcards.)

# LET'S PRACTICE

Write five letters of the Greek alphabet in order.

α  β  γ  δ  ε

Look at the Greek letter in the corner of each box. Find that letter in the words and circle it.

| α | ἀγάπην<br>ἀνήρ<br>ἄλλαι | β | βάτου<br>βόσκω<br>βίβλου |
|---|---|---|---|
| γ | γέγοναν<br>γίνομαι<br>γράφω | δ | διδάσκω<br>δίδωμι<br>διώκω |

☐ I practiced my flashcards today.

# LET'S PRACTICE

Color the boxes orange if the letters match the letter in the larger box at the beginning of each row.

| α | β | α | α | α |
|---|---|---|---|---|
|   | δ | α | γ | β |
| β | β | γ | β | β |
|   | ε | β | α | γ |
| γ | γ | γ | δ | α |
|   | β | α | γ | γ |
| δ | δ | ε | δ | δ |
|   | α | δ | δ | γ |
| ε | α | ε | ε | δ |
|   | β | ε | δ | ε |

☐ I practiced my flashcards today.

Lesson 6

# ZETA

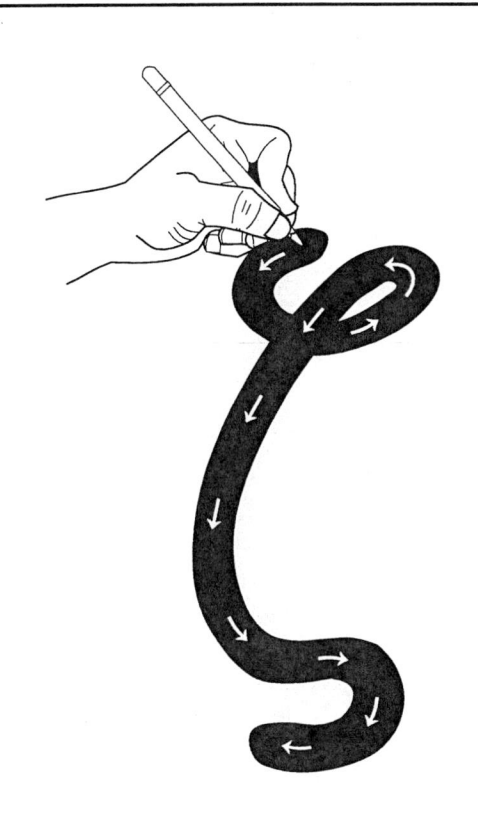

Write the letter *zeta* across each line.
As you write it, say "**zay**-ta."

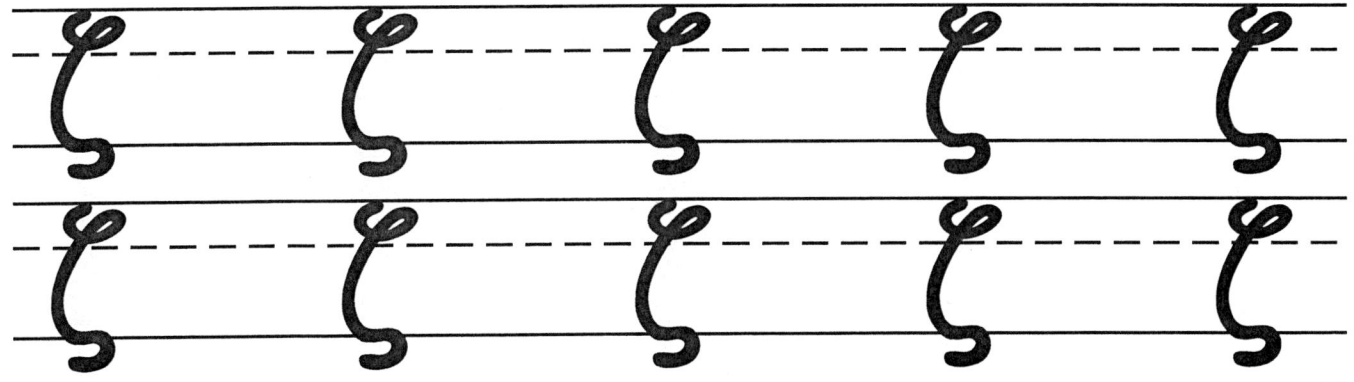

Greek Workbook - Level 1
Copyright © 1994 by Karen Mohs

# More Practice with ZETA

**Zeta sounds like dz in *adze*.**

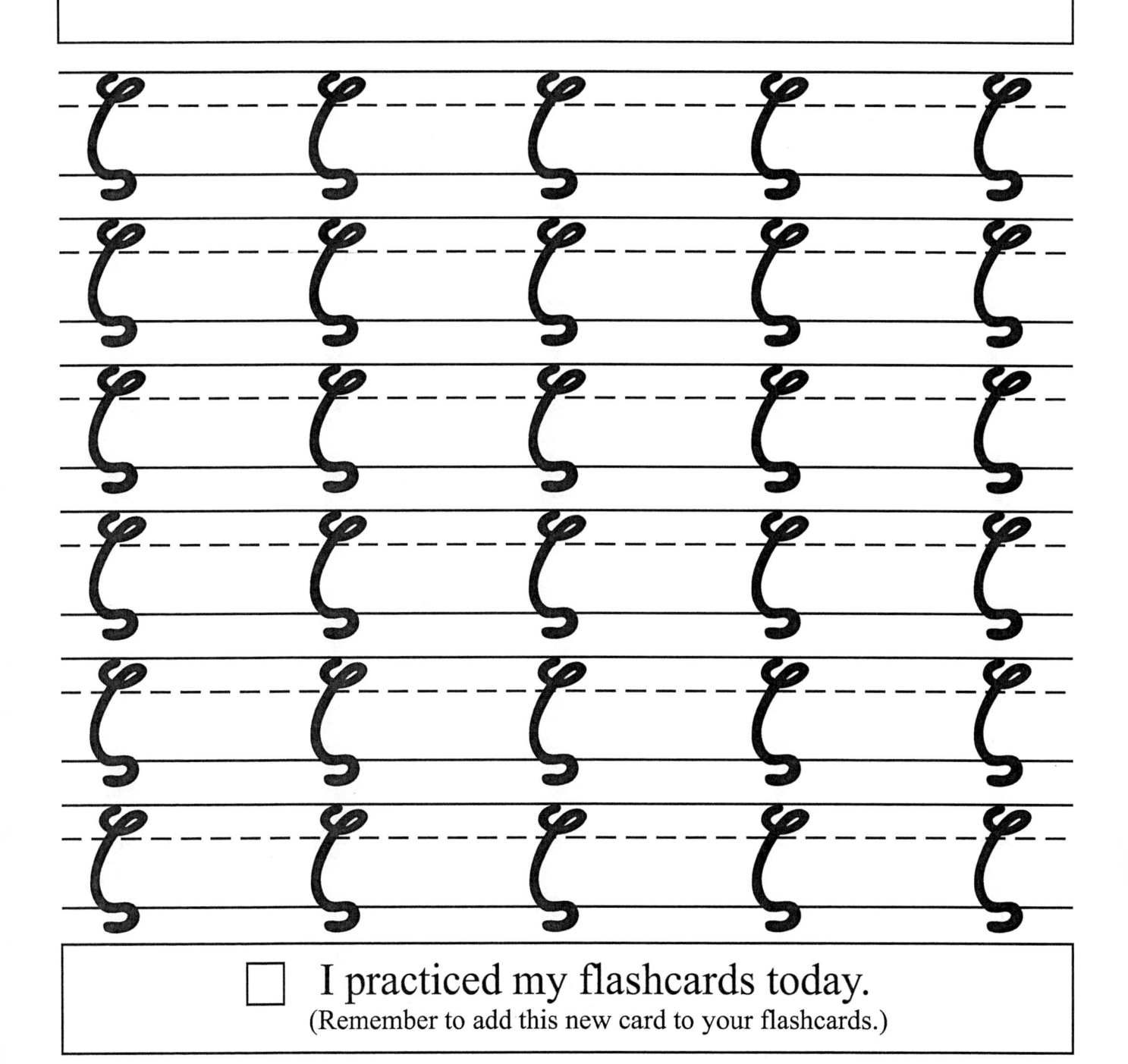

☐ I practiced my flashcards today.
(Remember to add this new card to your flashcards.)

# LET'S PRACTICE

Write six letters of the Greek alphabet in order.

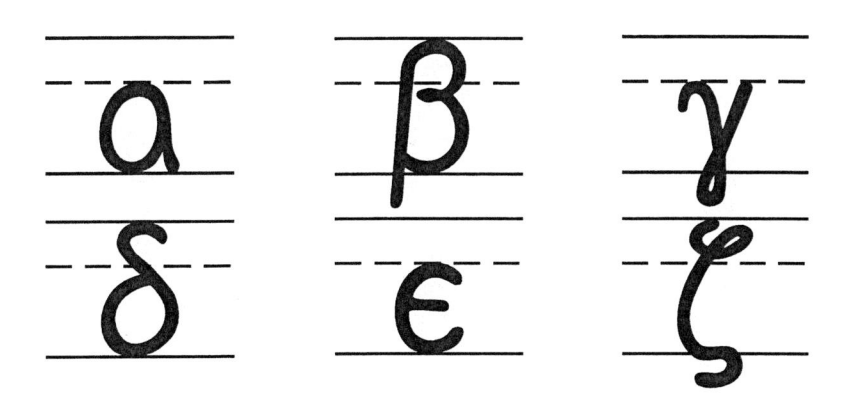

α  β  γ
δ  ε  ζ

Write the names of the Greek letters.

α   alpha

β   beta

γ   gamma

δ   delta

ε   epsilon

ζ   zeta

☐  I practiced my flashcards today.

# LET'S PRACTICE

Look at the boxes. Circle the Greek letters that are the same in each box.

| | | | |
|---|---|---|---|
| α β γ α | ζ β ε β | γ γ δ α | β δ δ ε |
| δ ζ ε ε | ζ β ζ δ | δ δ γ ζ | α ε β β |
| δ α α ε | γ ε α γ | β ε ε ζ | ζ ζ γ α |
| ε ε ζ γ | α δ α ε | δ α γ δ | ζ β β α |

☐ I practiced my flashcards today.

Greek Workbook - Level 1
Copyright © 1994 by Karen Mohs

Lesson 7

# ETA

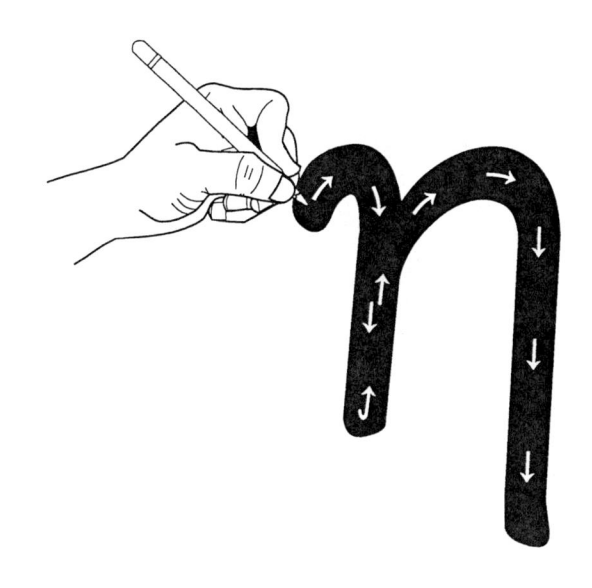

Write the letter *eta* across each line.
As you write it, say "**ay**-ta."

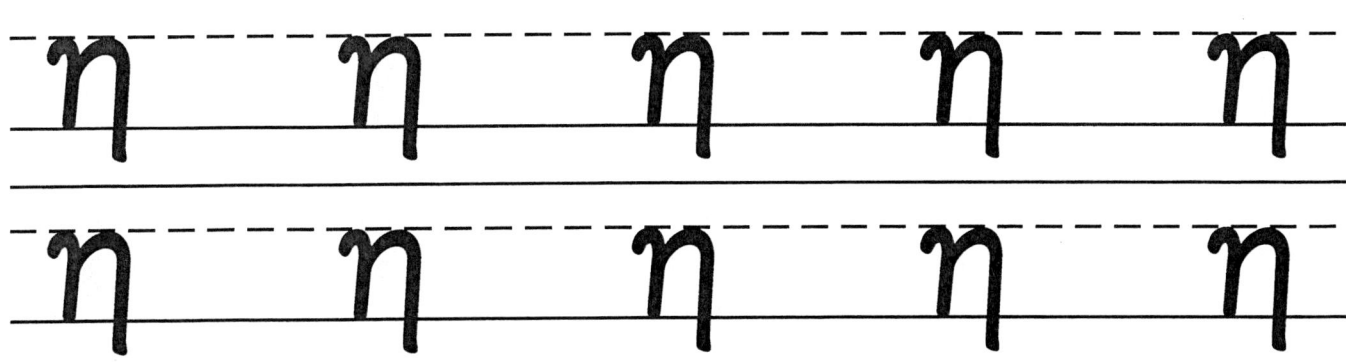

η   η   η   η   η

η   η   η   η   η

Greek Workbook - Level 1
Copyright © 1994 by Karen Mohs

# More Practice with ETA

Eta sounds like **a** in *late*.

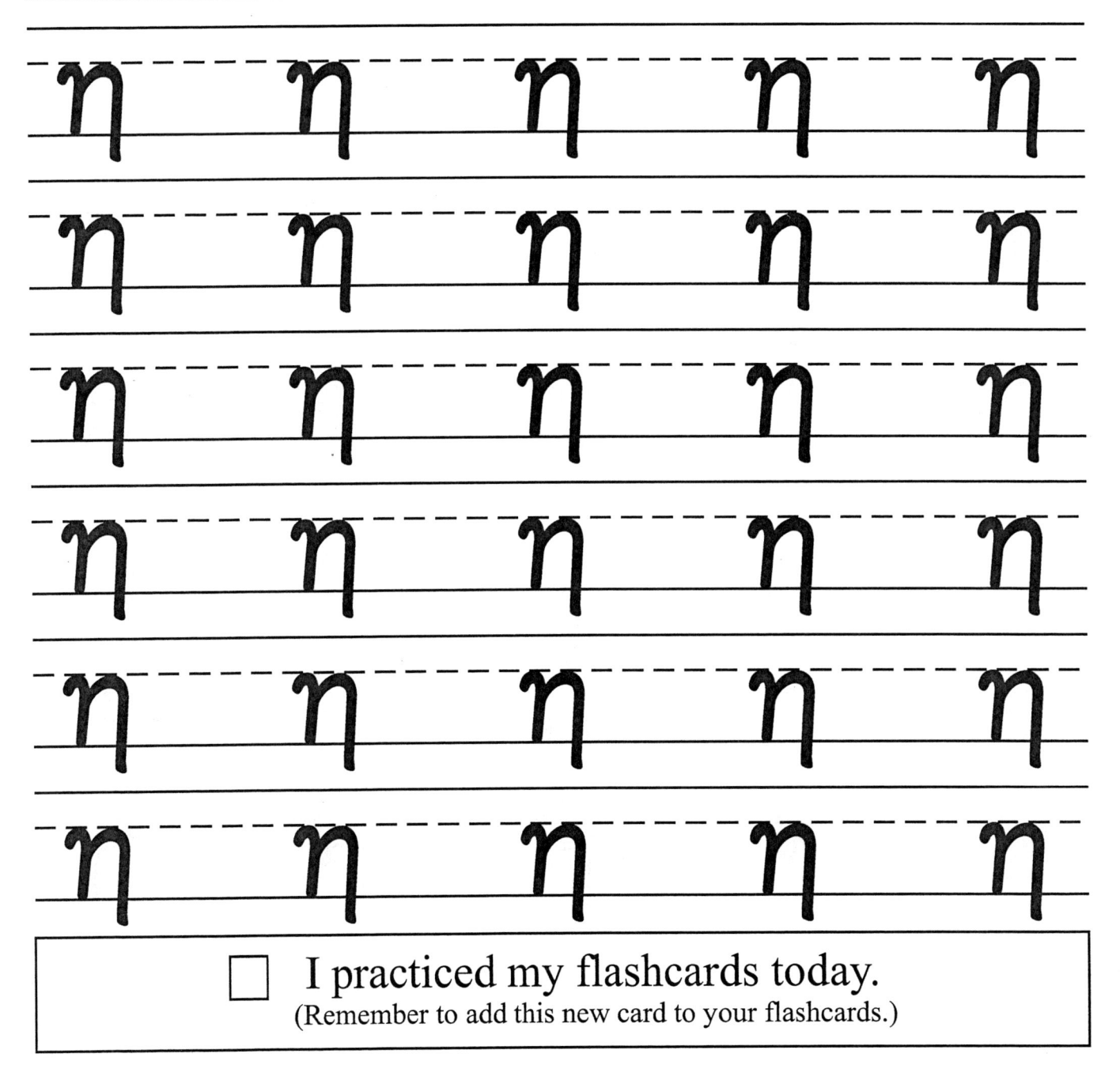

η η η η η

η η η η η

η η η η η

η η η η η

η η η η η

η η η η η

☐ I practiced my flashcards today.
(Remember to add this new card to your flashcards.)

# LET'S PRACTICE

Write seven letters of the Greek alphabet in order.

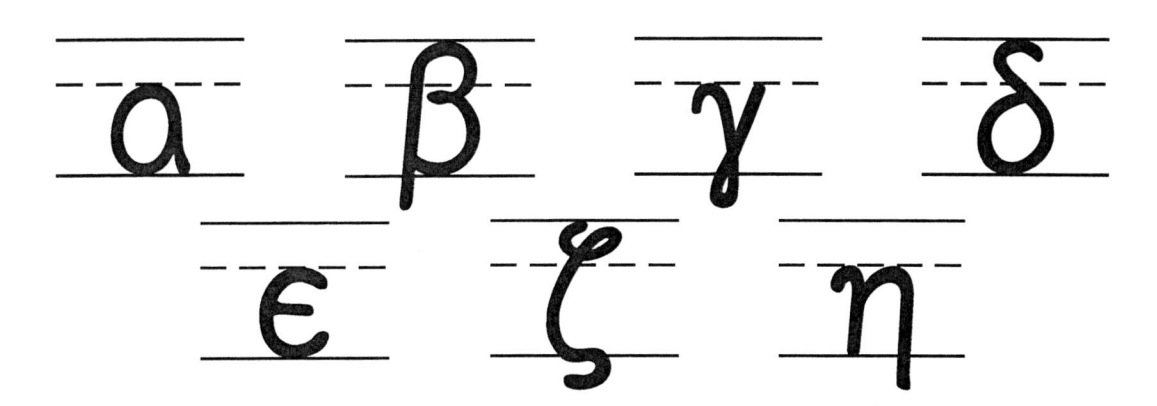

α   β   γ   δ

ε   ζ   η

Circle the name of the Greek letter at the beginning of each row.

| | | | |
|---|---|---|---|
| δ | (delta) | beta | epsilon |
| η | zeta | gamma | (eta) |
| α | eta | (alpha) | gamma |
| ε | eta | (epsilon) | zeta |
| β | alpha | delta | (beta) |
| ζ | (zeta) | delta | alpha |
| γ | beta | (gamma) | epsilon |

☐ I practiced my flashcards today.

# LET'S PRACTICE

Color the triangle if the letter name matches the Greek letter at the top.

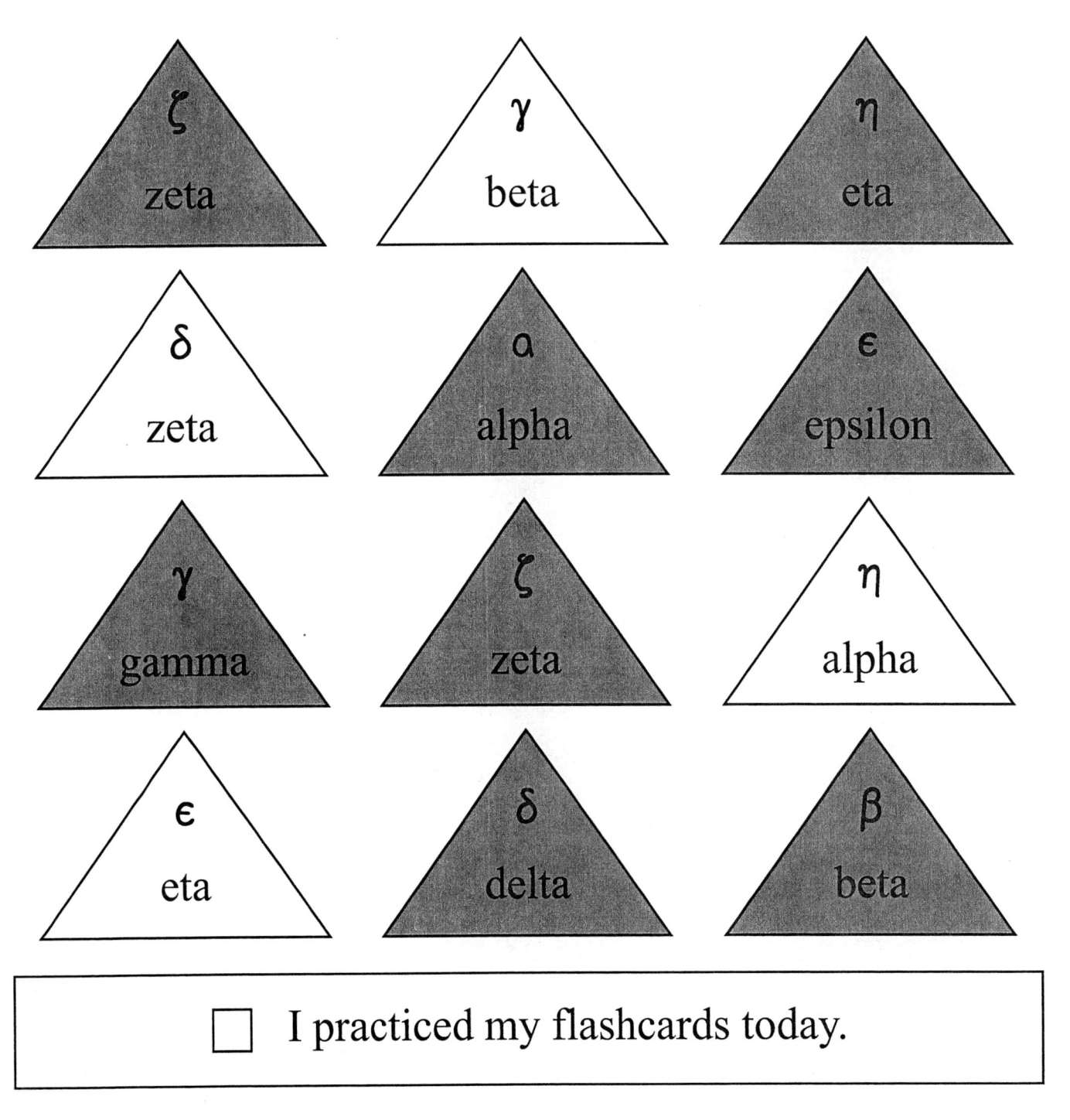

| ζ — zeta (colored) | γ — beta | η — eta (colored) |
| δ — zeta | α — alpha (colored) | ε — epsilon (colored) |
| γ — gamma (colored) | ζ — zeta (colored) | η — alpha |
| ε — eta | δ — delta (colored) | β — beta (colored) |

☐ I practiced my flashcards today.

Lesson 8

# THETA

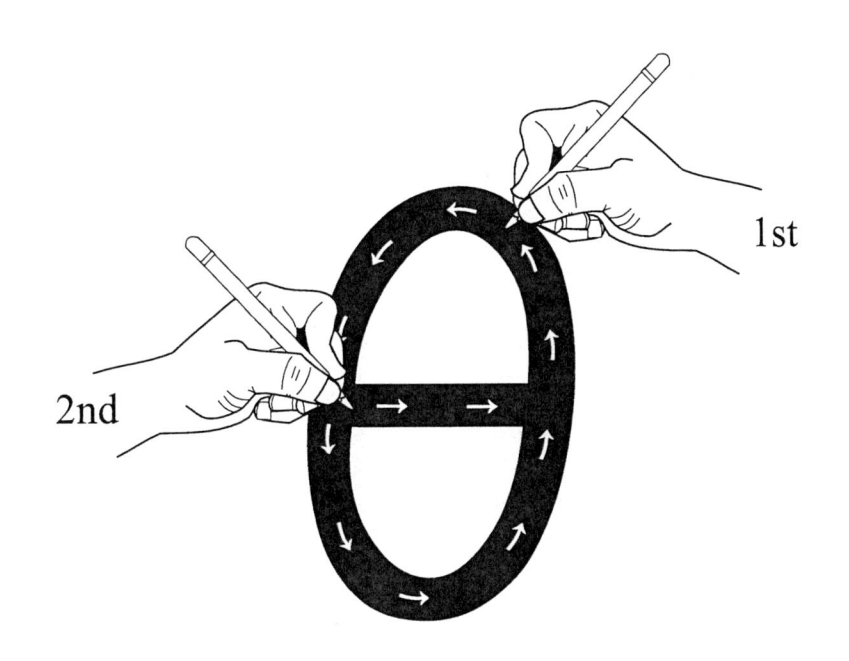

Write the letter *theta* across each line.
As you write it, say "**thay**-ta."

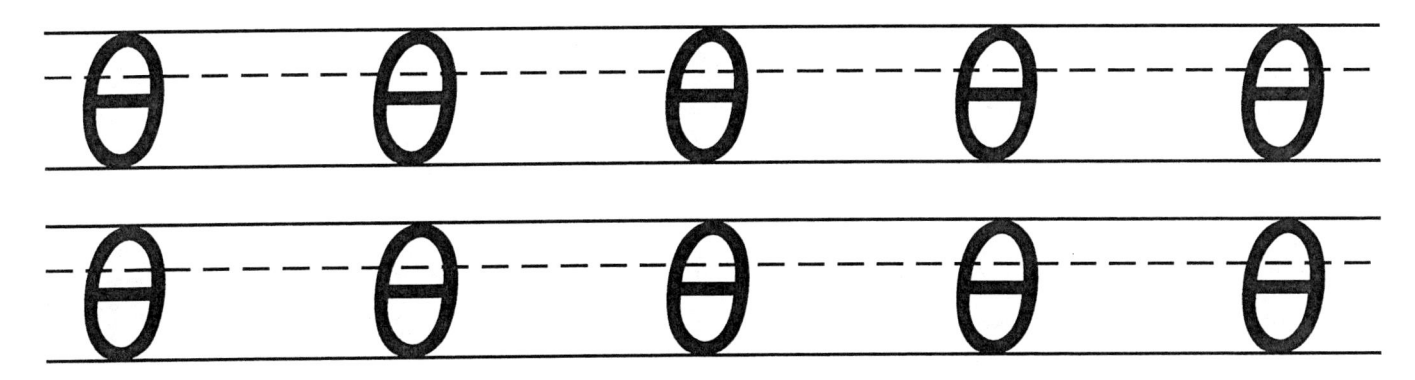

Greek Workbook - Level 1
Copyright © 1994 by Karen Mohs

# More Practice with THETA

Theta sounds like **th** in *bath*.

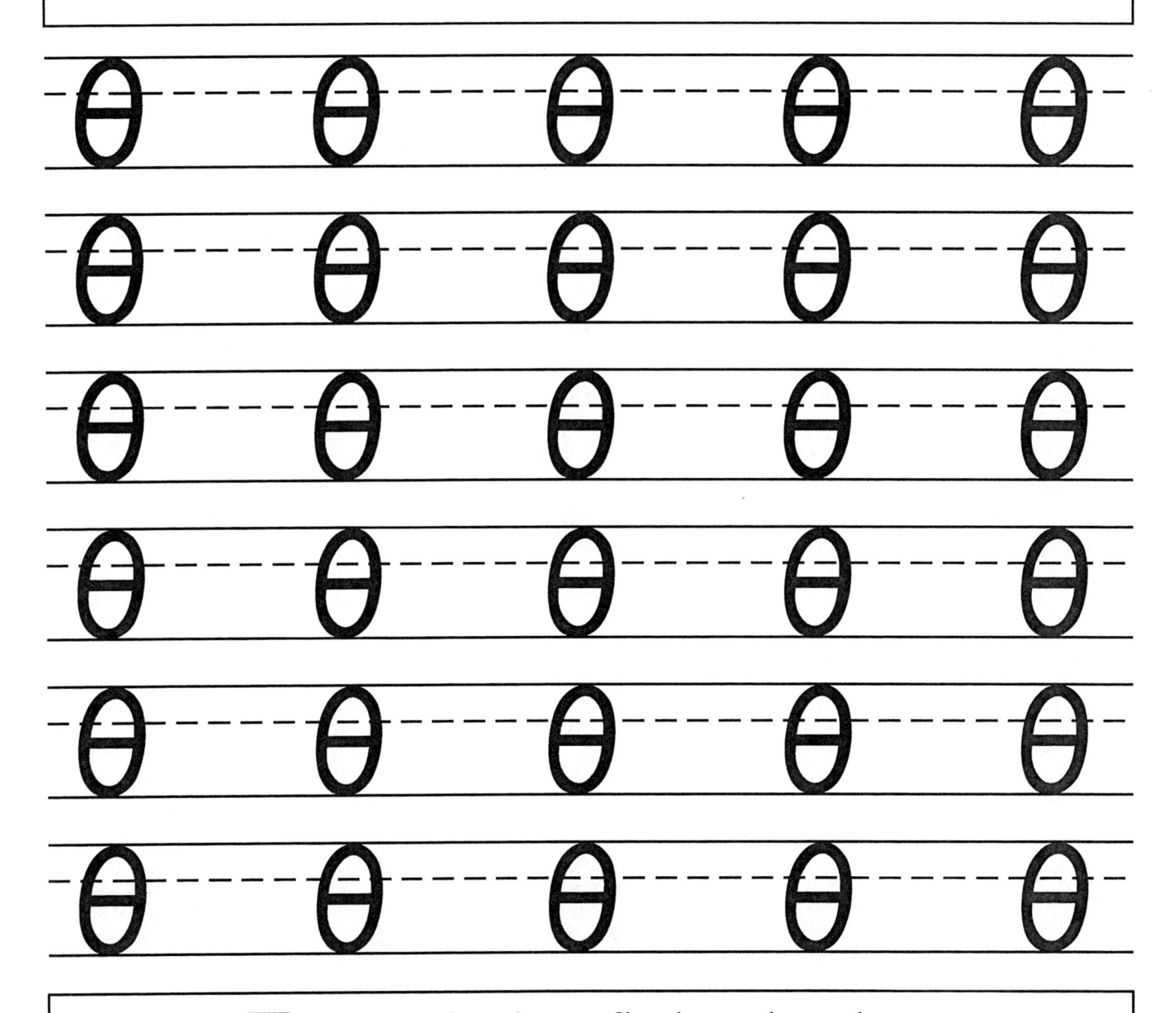

θ θ θ θ θ

θ θ θ θ θ

θ θ θ θ θ

θ θ θ θ θ

θ θ θ θ θ

θ θ θ θ θ

☐ I practiced my flashcards today.
(Remember to add this new card to your flashcards.)

# LET'S PRACTICE

Write eight letters of the Greek alphabet in order.

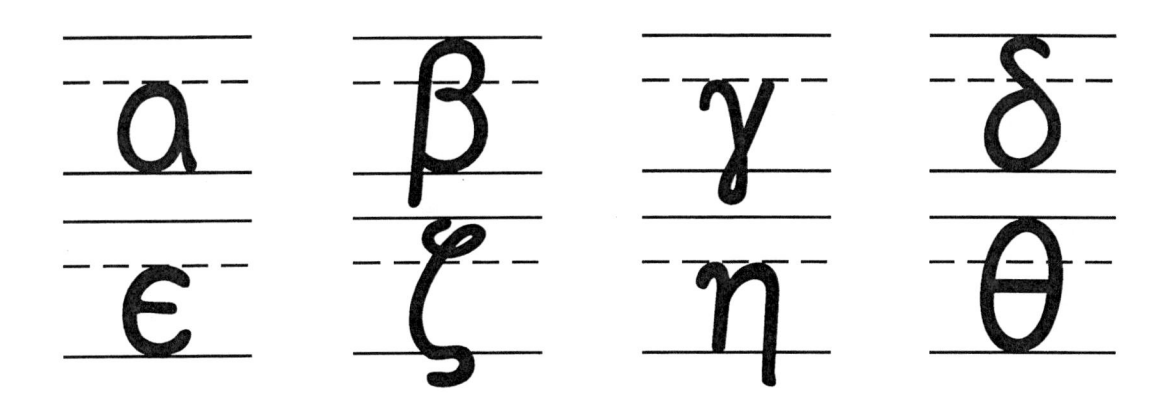

α  β  γ  δ
ε  ζ  η  θ

Read the letter names in the big boxes. Circle all the Greek letters that belong to each name.

| gamma | β | ε | α | ⓖ | ⓖ | ε | ⓖ | δ | δ |
|---|---|---|---|---|---|---|---|---|---|
| epsilon | ⓔ | η | η | ⓔ | ζ | η | α | θ | ⓔ |
| eta | θ | ⓗ | ε | α | ε | ε | ⓗ | ζ | ⓗ |
| beta | γ | α | ⓑ | γ | ⓑ | η | δ | ⓑ | γ |
| zeta | ⓩ | δ | ε | δ | α | ⓩ | δ | ε | ⓩ |
| theta | γ | β | ⓣ | ⓣ | δ | β | ⓣ | γ | β |
| delta | α | ⓓ | ζ | β | ⓓ | ζ | ζ | ⓓ | β |

☐ I practiced my flashcards today.

Greek Workbook - Level 1
Copyright © 1994 by Karen Mohs

# LET'S PRACTICE

Draw stems on the flowers to put them in their own vases.

alpha | beta | gamma | delta | epsilon | zeta | eta | theta

☐ I practiced my flashcards today.

Lesson 9

# IOTA

Write the letter *iota* across each line.
As you write it, say "ee-**o**-ta."

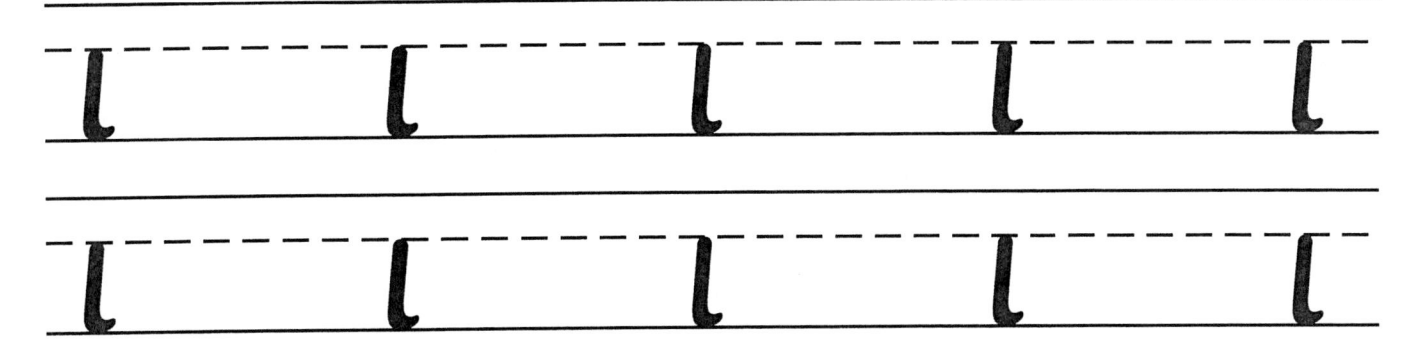

# More Practice with IOTA

*Iota sounds like **i** in pit.*

ι ι ι ι ι

ι ι ι ι ι

ι ι ι ι ι

ι ι ι ι ι

ι ι ι ι ι

ι ι ι ι ι

☐ I practiced my flashcards today.
(Remember to add this new card to your flashcards.)

# LET'S PRACTICE

Write nine letters of the Greek alphabet in order.

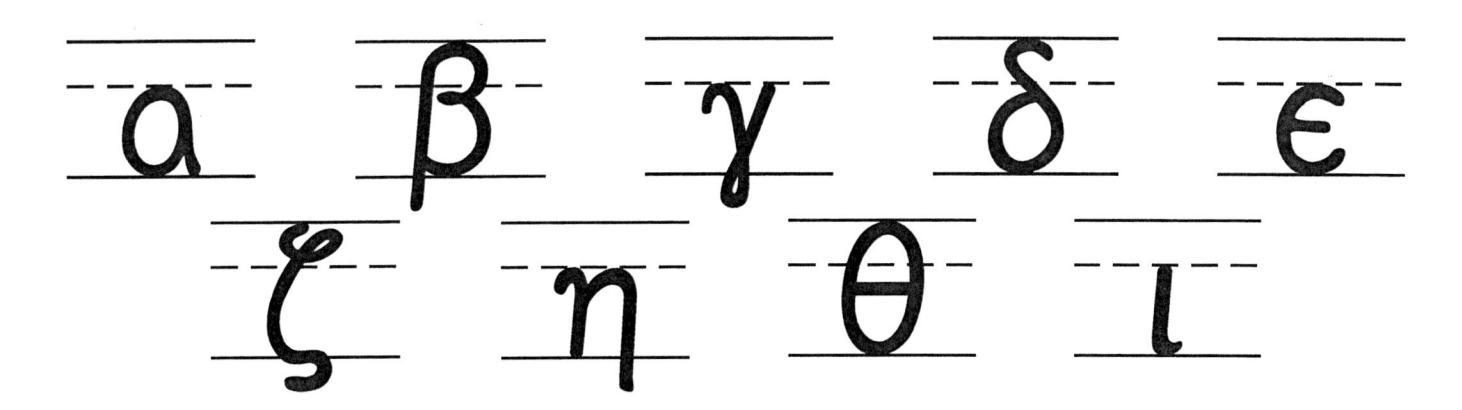

α   β   γ   δ   ε
ζ   η   θ   ι

Circle the correct letter names below the Greek letters.

| θ || ε || β ||
|---|---|---|---|---|---|
| eta | (theta) | (epsilon) | delta | zeta | (beta) |
| δ || α || η ||
| (delta) | iota | theta | (alpha) | beta | (eta) |
| ζ || ι || γ ||
| gamma | (zeta) | (iota) | alpha | (gamma) | epsilon |

☐ I practiced my flashcards today.

# LET'S PRACTICE

Circle the words that have the same sound as the Greek letter at the beginning of each row.

| | | | |
|---|---|---|---|
| δ | (date) | tent | blue |
| | sun | (dog) | bus |
| ι | (miss) | tool | rag |
| | coat | pray | (bin) |
| η | home | risk | (cape) |
| | pipe | (same) | stem |
| γ | sack | (good) | way |
| | (Greek) | rain | (tug) |
| θ | open | queen | (math) |
| | orange | (bath) | quit |
| ζ | (adze) | (odds) | fish |
| | dog | fork | bend |
| ε | cat | shoe | (red) |
| | (wet) | mice | yam |

☐ I practiced my flashcards today.

Lesson 10

# KAPPA

Write the letter *kappa* across each line.
As you write it, say "**kap**-pa."

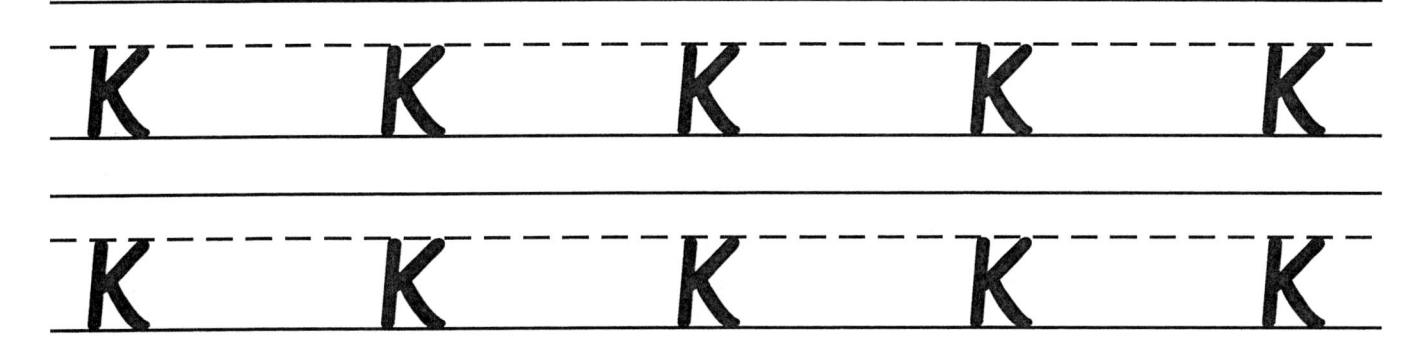

K  K  K  K  K

K  K  K  K  K

# More Practice with KAPPA

Kappa sounds like **k** in *kite*.

K K K K K

K K K K K

K K K K K

K K K K K

K K K K K

K K K K K

☐ I practiced my flashcards today.
(Remember to add this new card to your flashcards.)

# LET'S PRACTICE

Write ten letters of the Greek alphabet in order.

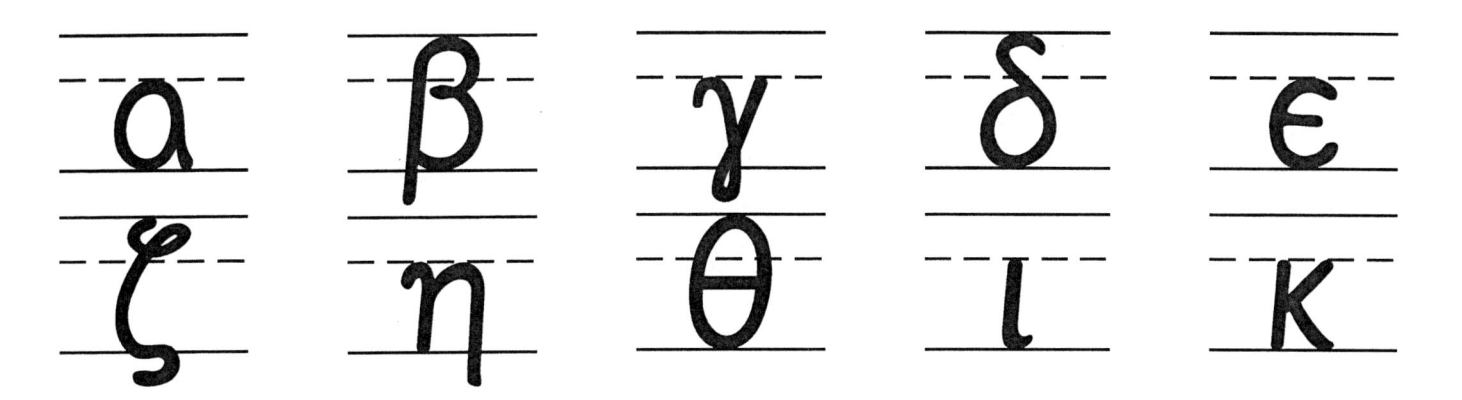

α  β  γ  δ  ε
ζ  η  θ  ι  κ

Look at the Greek letter at the top of each box. Find that letter in the words below and circle it.

| ι | δ | ζ | κ |
|---|---|---|---|
| ἰδίων<br>βιβλίον<br>ἰσχύν | δέω<br>δίδωμι<br>δολόω | ζόφον<br>ζώνη<br>ζήλου | καθότι<br>κέκληκε<br>κόκκον |

| θ | ε | γ | η |
|---|---|---|---|
| θέσθε<br>θηρίον<br>θύρα | ἔχω<br>ἑτέρου<br>εὑρέθη | γογγύζω<br>γραφή<br>γυνή | ἠνοίγη<br>ἤχθη<br>ἥκω |

☐ I practiced my flashcards today.

# LET'S PRACTICE

Tick-Tack-Toe!
Draw lines through three Greek letters that are alike.

Lesson 11

# LAMBDA

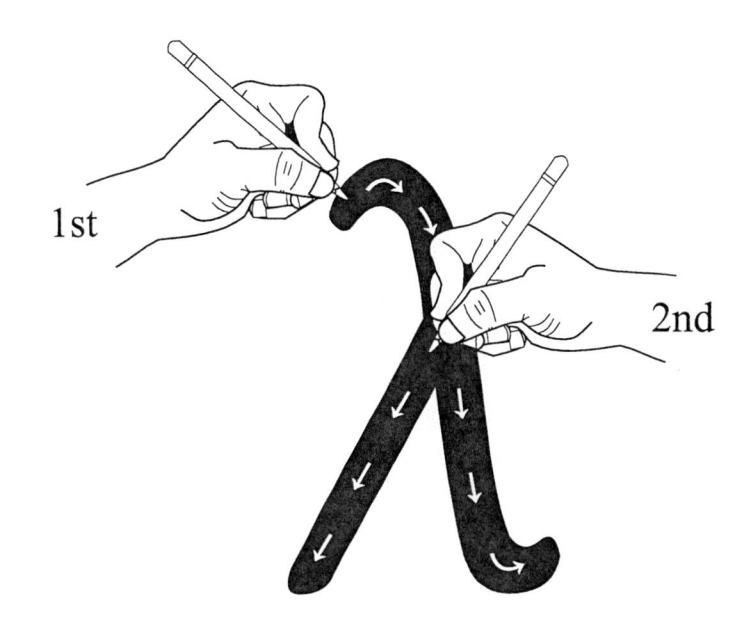

Write the letter *lambda* across each line.
As you write it, say "**lamb**-da."

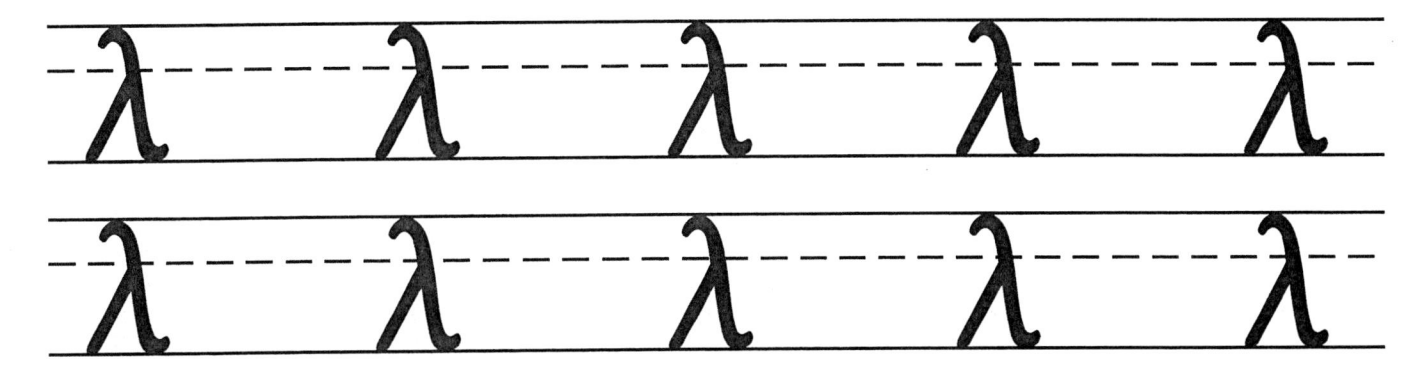

λ   λ   λ   λ   λ

λ   λ   λ   λ   λ

Greek Workbook - Level 1
Copyright © 1994 by Karen Mohs

41

# More Practice with LAMBDA

Lambda sounds like **l** in *lamb*.

λ  λ  λ  λ  λ

λ  λ  λ  λ  λ

λ  λ  λ  λ  λ

λ  λ  λ  λ  λ

λ  λ  λ  λ  λ

λ  λ  λ  λ  λ

☐ I practiced my flashcards today.
(Remember to add this new card to your flashcards.)

# LET'S PRACTICE

Write eleven letters of the Greek alphabet in order.

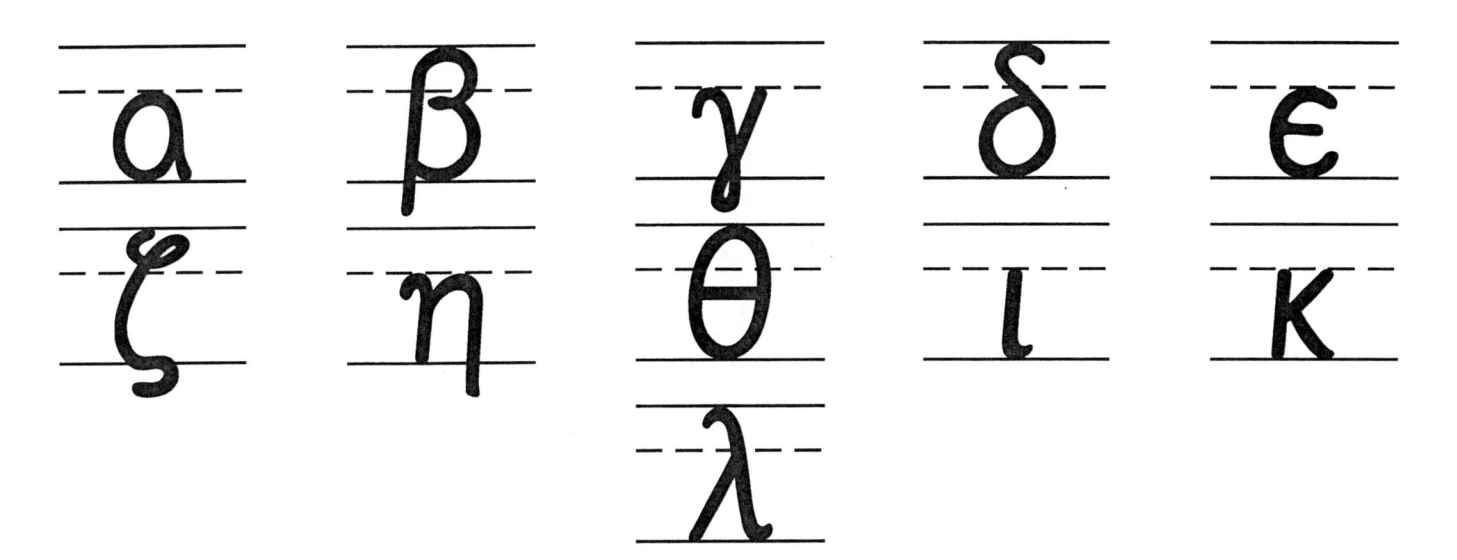

α  β  γ  δ  ε
ζ  η  θ  ι  κ
      λ

Look at the circled letter in each box. Which Greek letter comes next? Circle it.

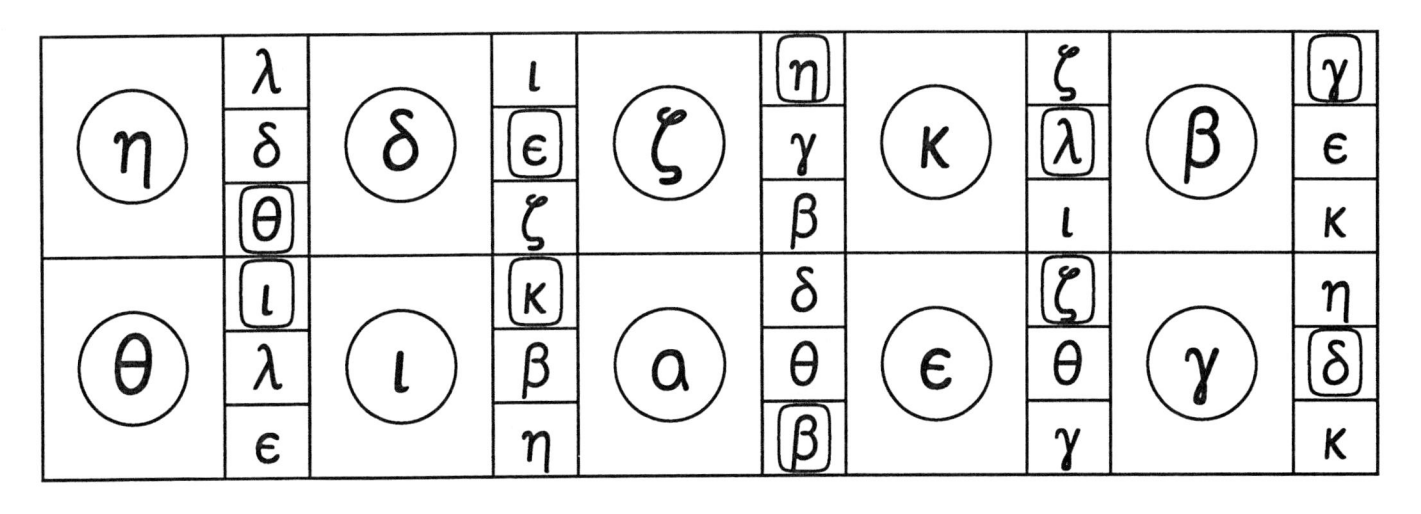

| ⓗ | λ<br>δ<br>θ | ⓓ | ι<br>ε<br>ζ | ⓩ | η<br>γ<br>β | ⓚ | ζ<br>λ<br>ι | ⓑ | γ<br>ε<br>κ |
|---|---|---|---|---|---|---|---|---|---|
| ⓞ | ι<br>λ<br>ε | ⓘ | κ<br>β<br>η | ⓐ | δ<br>θ<br>β | ⓔ | ζ<br>θ<br>γ | ⓖ | η<br>δ<br>κ |

☐ I practiced my flashcards today.

# LET'S PRACTICE

Circle the correct names of the Greek letters.

| beta    epsilon<br>θ<br>lambda   (theta) | alpha    eta<br>ε<br>(epsilon)   zeta | theta    alpha<br>β<br>kappa    (beta) |
|---|---|---|
| eta    delta<br>κ<br>(kappa)   lambda | (lambda)  gamma<br>λ<br>alpha    zeta | iota    (eta)<br>η<br>gamma   epsilon |
| lambda   (delta)<br>δ<br>beta    zeta | (gamma)   delta<br>γ<br>kappa    theta | epsilon   lambda<br>ι<br>(iota)    alpha |
| theta   (alpha)<br>α<br>gamma    kappa | delta    beta<br>ζ<br>iota    (zeta) | (lambda)   delta<br>λ<br>iota    gamma |

☐ I practiced my flashcards today.

Lesson 12

# MU

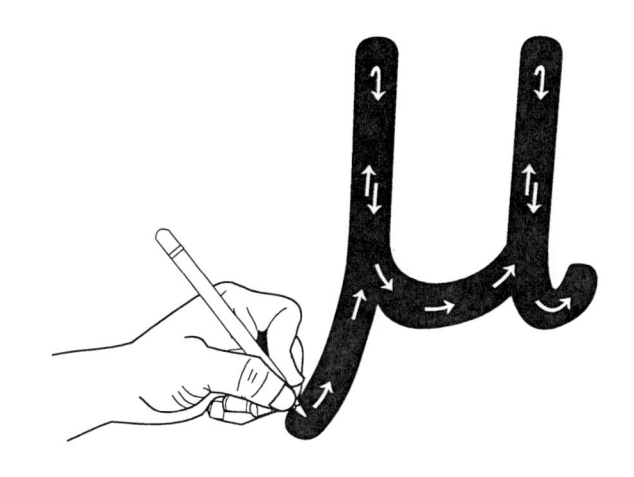

Write the letter *mu* across each line.
As you write it, say **"moo."**

μ   μ   μ   μ   μ

μ   μ   μ   μ   μ

Greek Workbook - Level 1
Copyright © 1994 by Karen Mohs

# More Practice with MU

**Mu sounds like m in *man*.**

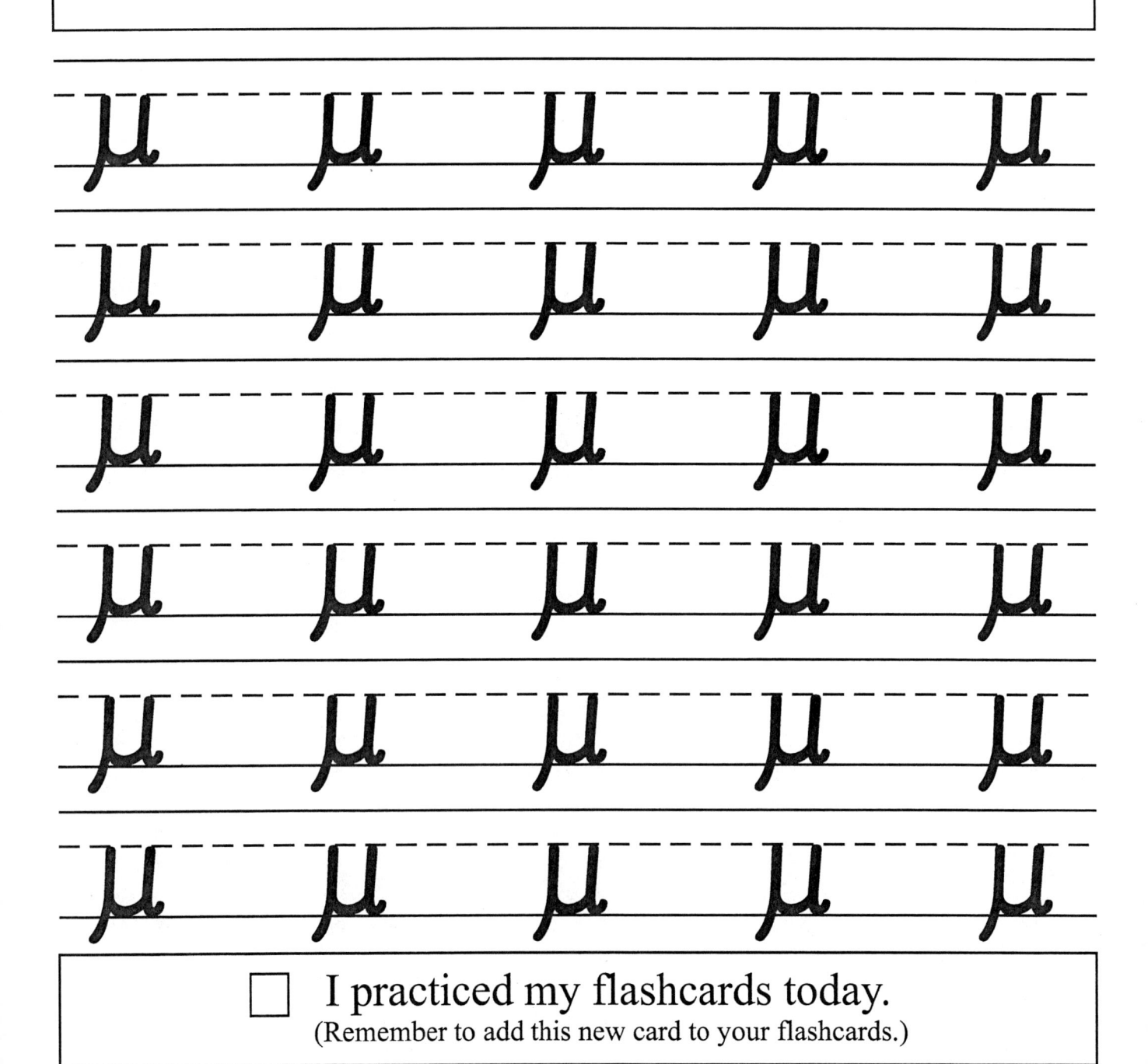

μ μ μ μ μ

μ μ μ μ μ

μ μ μ μ μ

μ μ μ μ μ

μ μ μ μ μ

μ μ μ μ μ

☐ I practiced my flashcards today.
(Remember to add this new card to your flashcards.)

# LET'S PRACTICE

Write twelve letters of the Greek alphabet in order.

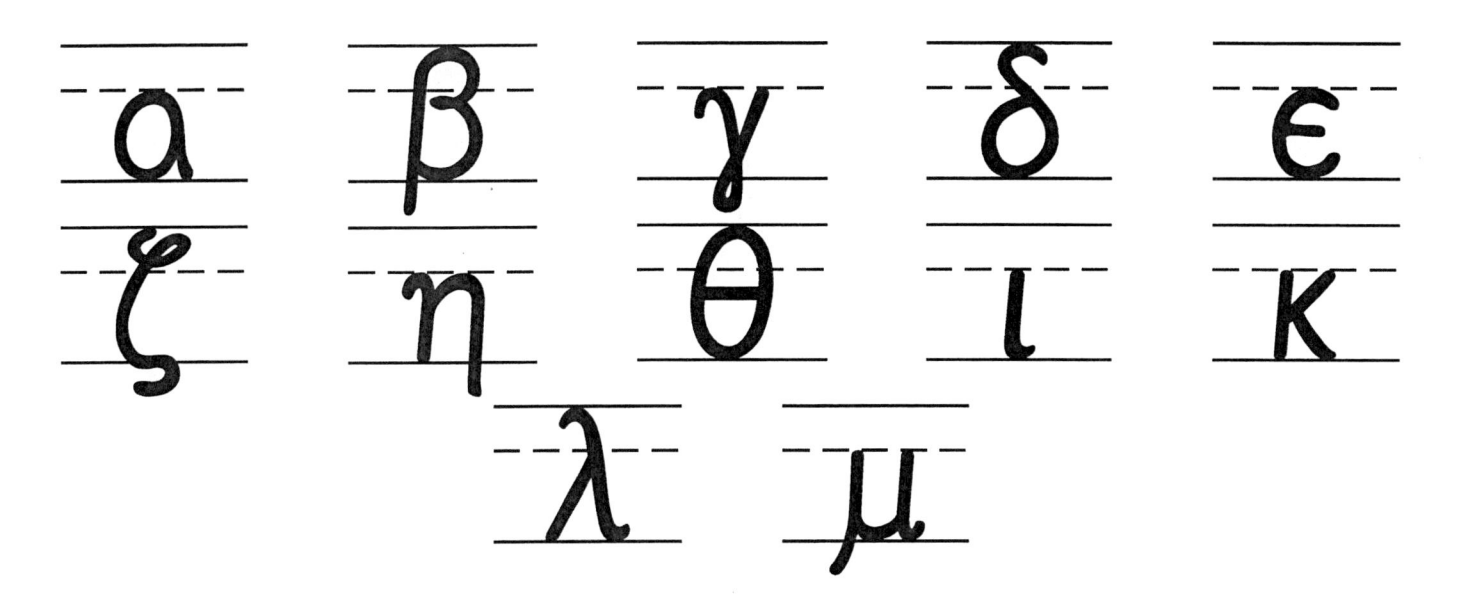

α  β  γ  δ  ε
ζ  η  θ  ι  κ
      λ  μ

Draw lines from the Greek letters to their names.

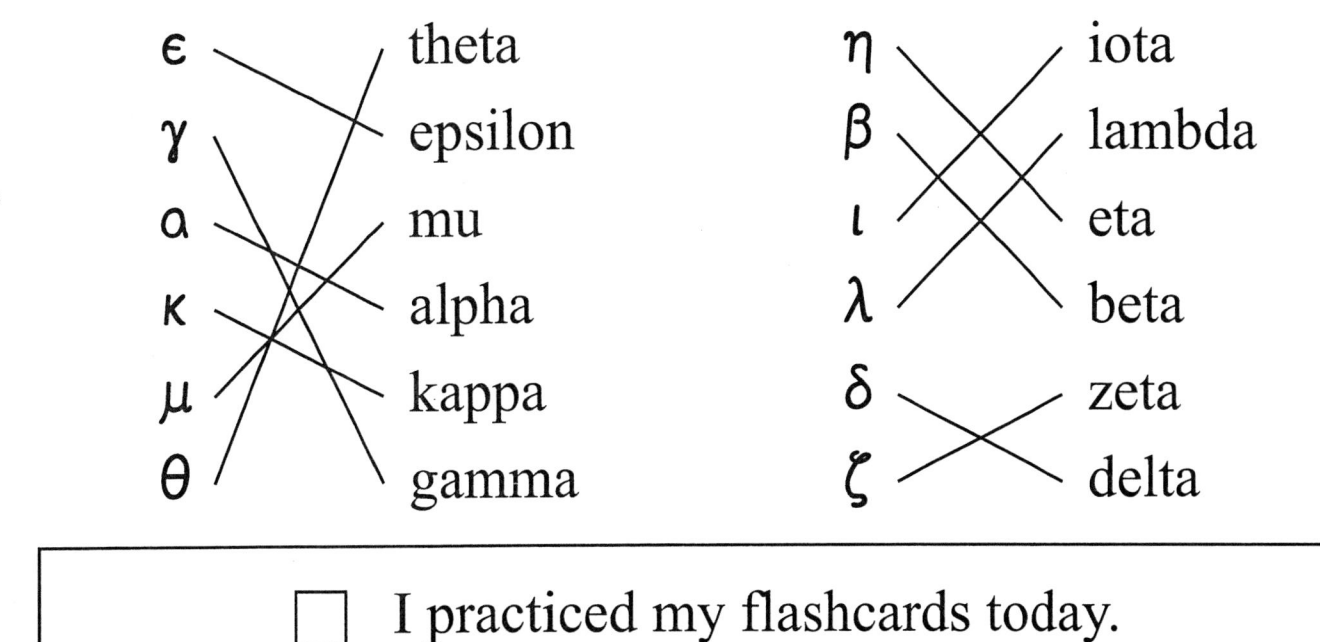

ε — epsilon
γ — gamma
α — alpha
κ — kappa
μ — mu
θ — theta

η — eta
β — beta
ι — iota
λ — lambda
δ — delta
ζ — zeta

☐ I practiced my flashcards today.

# LET'S PRACTICE

Write the correct Greek letters on the lines.

| gamma | γ | kappa | κ | zeta | ζ |
| --- | --- | --- | --- | --- | --- |
| alpha | α | iota | ι | epsilon | ε |
| mu | μ | theta | θ | delta | δ |
| lambda | λ | eta | η | beta | β |

Which letters go below the line?

β    γ    ζ    η    μ

Which letters are tall?

β    δ    ζ    θ    λ

☐ I practiced my flashcards today.

Lesson 13

# NU

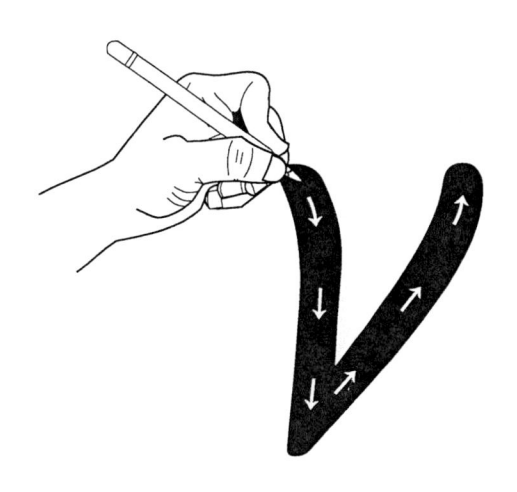

Write the letter *nu* across each line.
As you write it, say **"noo."**

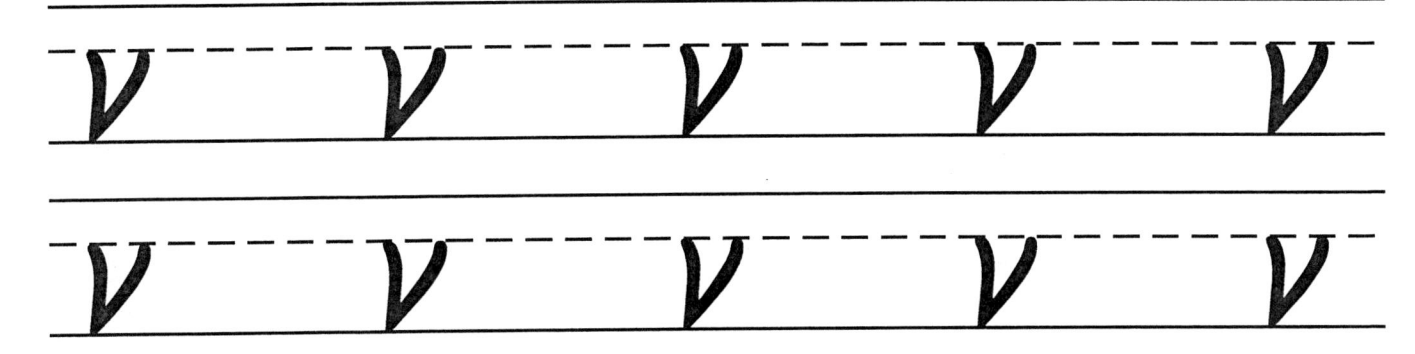

ν  ν  ν  ν  ν

ν  ν  ν  ν  ν

# More Practice with NU

Nu sounds like **n** in *nice*.

ν ν ν ν ν

ν ν ν ν ν

ν ν ν ν ν

ν ν ν ν ν

ν ν ν ν ν

ν ν ν ν ν

☐ I practiced my flashcards today.
(Remember to add this new card to your flashcards.)

# LET'S PRACTICE

Write thirteen letters of the Greek alphabet in order.

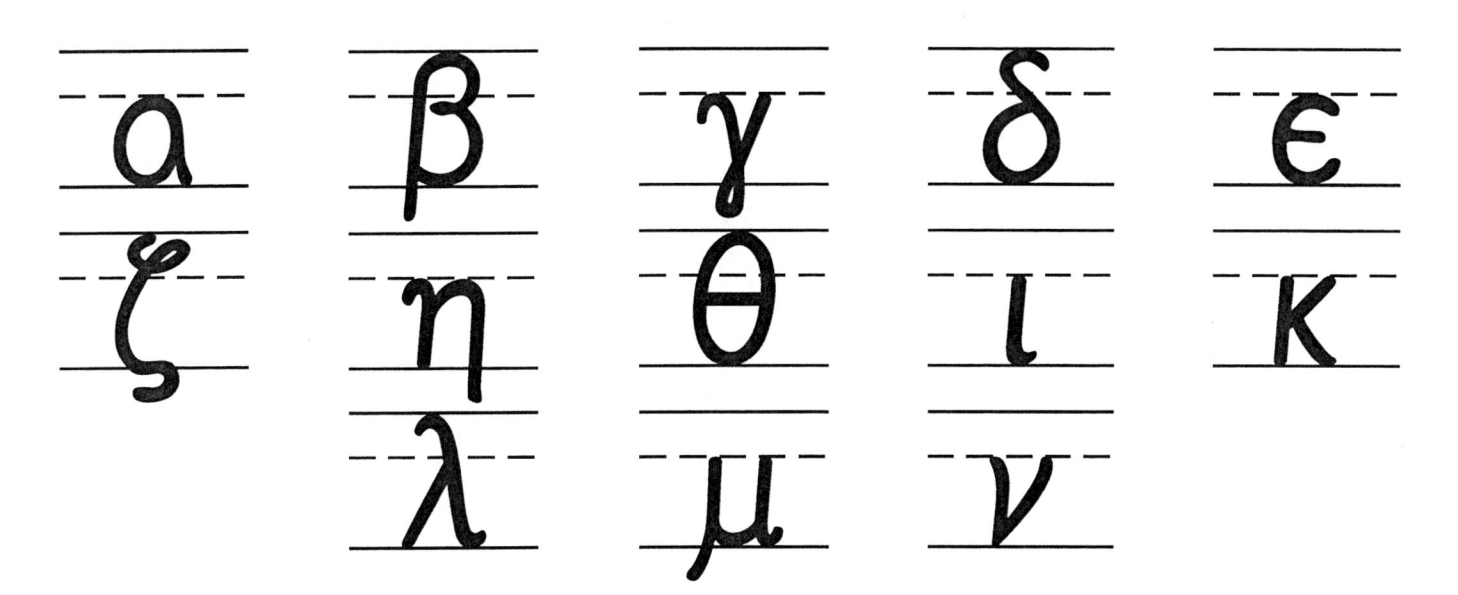

α   β   γ   δ   ε
ζ   η   θ   ι   κ
     λ   μ   ν

Connect the dots in the correct order.

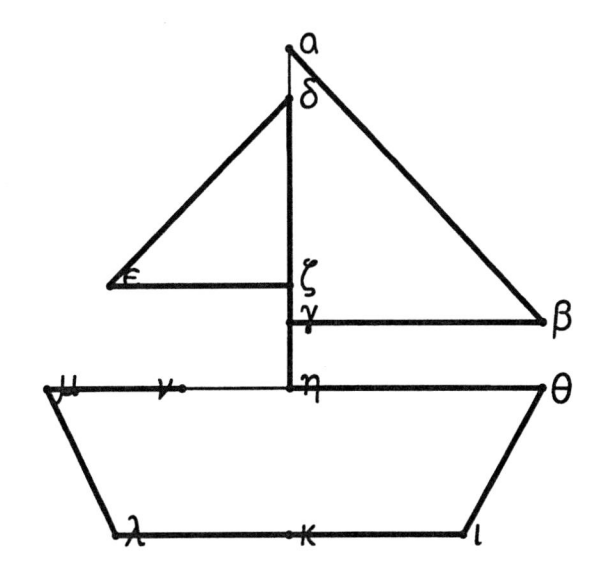

☐   I practiced my flashcards today.

# LET'S PRACTICE

Circle the correct Greek letters.

| | | | |
|---|---|---|---|
| lambda | θ | **(λ)** | α |
| eta | **(η)** | ε | ζ |
| theta | γ | δ | **(θ)** |
| kappa | η | ι | **(κ)** |
| mu | **(μ)** | β | λ |
| delta | ζ | **(δ)** | α |
| iota | ν | **(ι)** | β |
| epsilon | **(ε)** | η | ι |
| nu | κ | μ | **(ν)** |
| zeta | θ | **(ζ)** | γ |
| gamma | **(γ)** | κ | δ |

☐ I practiced my flashcards today.

Lesson 14

# XI

Write the letter *xi* across each line.
As you write it, say **"ksee."**

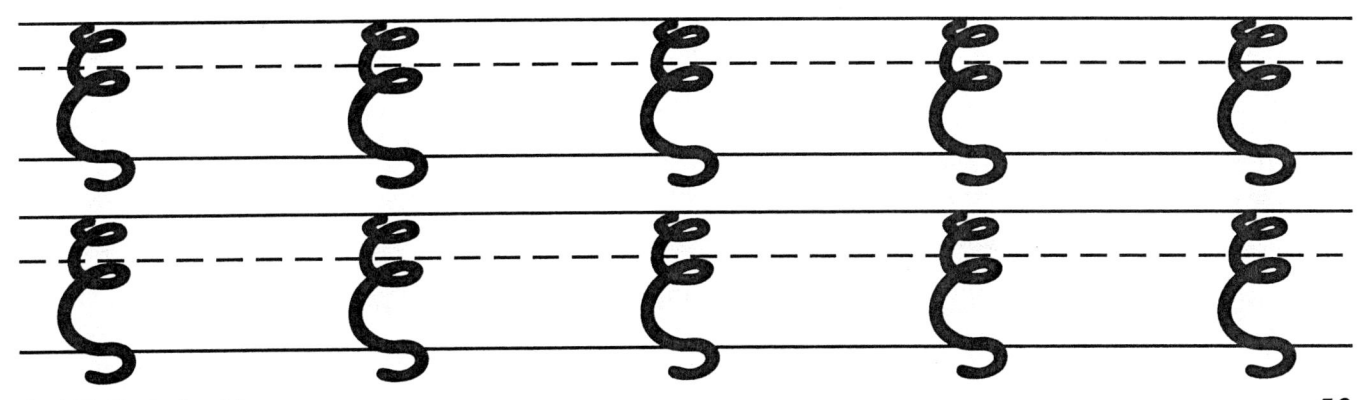

Greek Workbook - Level 1
Copyright © 1994 by Karen Mohs

53

# More Practice with XI

Xi sounds like **x** in *box*.

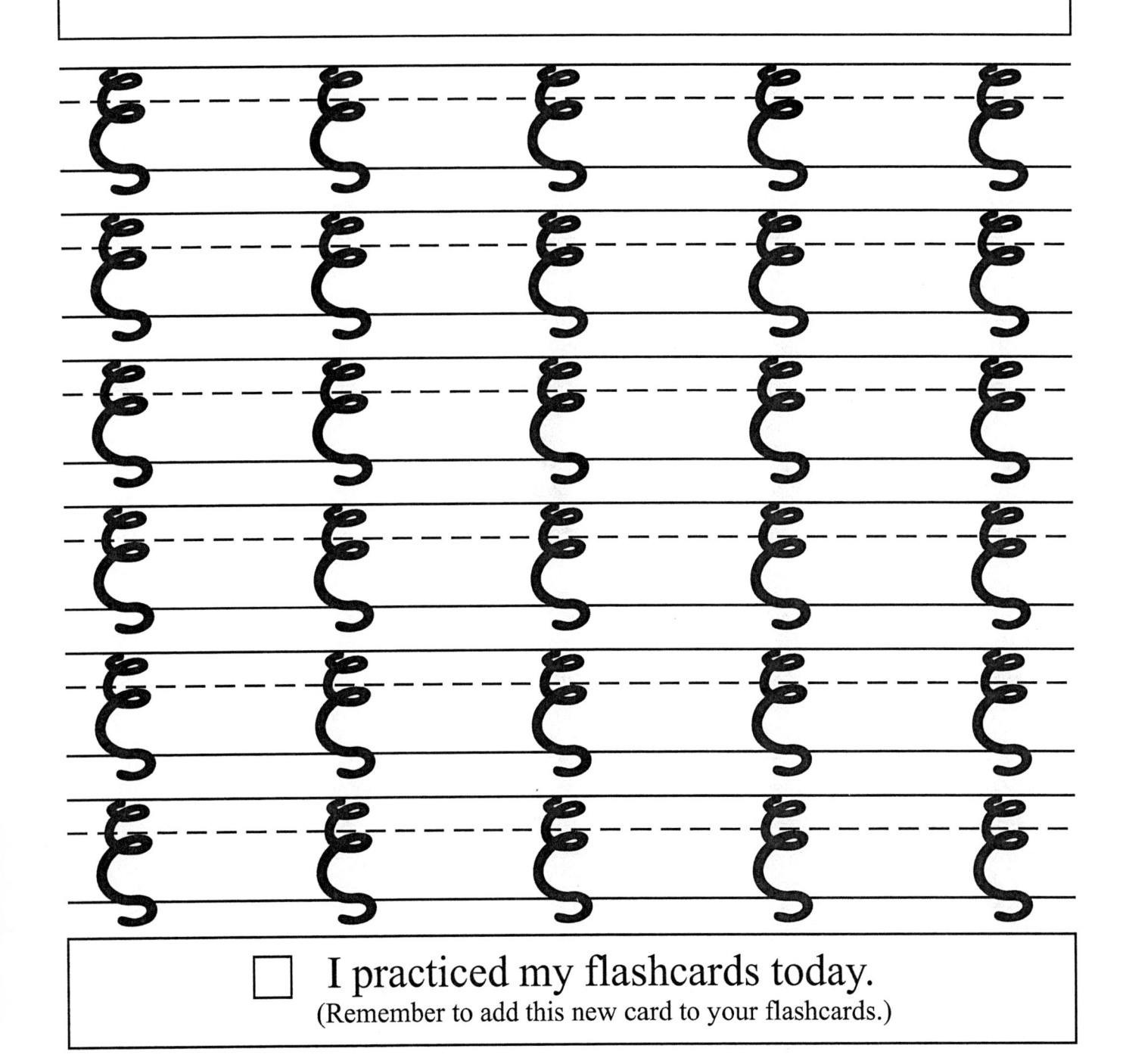

☐ I practiced my flashcards today.
(Remember to add this new card to your flashcards.)

# LET'S PRACTICE

Write fourteen letters of the Greek alphabet in order.

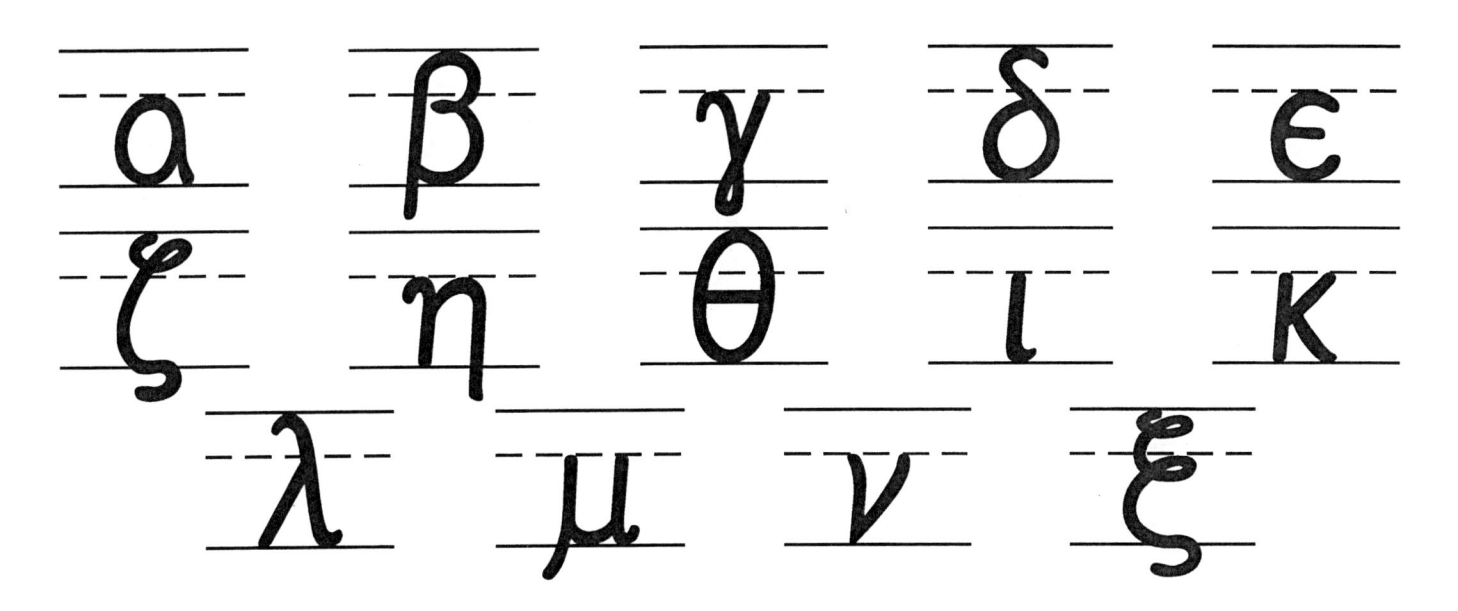

α  β  γ  δ  ε
ζ  η  θ  ι  κ
λ  μ  ν  ξ

Circle all the Greek letters you have learned so far.

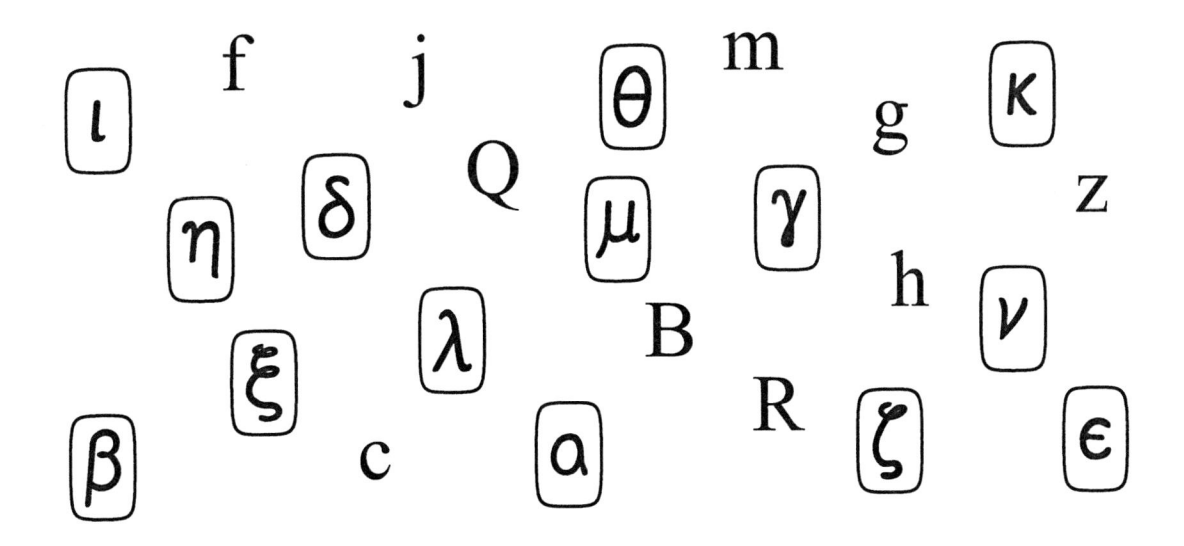

(ι)  f  j  (θ)  m  (κ)
(η) (δ)  Q  (μ)  (γ)  g  z
(ξ)  (λ)  B  h  (ν)
(β)  c  (α)  R  (ζ)  (ε)

☐ I practiced my flashcards today.

# LET'S PRACTICE

Circle the correct names of the Greek letters.

| | | | | | |
|---|---|---|---|---|---|
| β | (beta) / kappa / zeta | κ | alpha / eta / (kappa) | η | nu / (eta) / epsilon |
| λ | delta / gamma / (lambda) | ν | gamma / (nu) / lambda | ε | mu / iota / (epsilon) |
| μ | delta / (mu) / gamma | θ | gamma / (theta) / beta | ξ | lambda / (xi) / delta |
| ζ | beta / xi / (zeta) | ι | epsilon / (iota) / lambda | δ | (delta) / theta / kappa |

☐ I practiced my flashcards today.

Lesson 15

# OMICRON

Write the letter *omicron* across each line.
As you write it, say "**ahm**-i-cron."

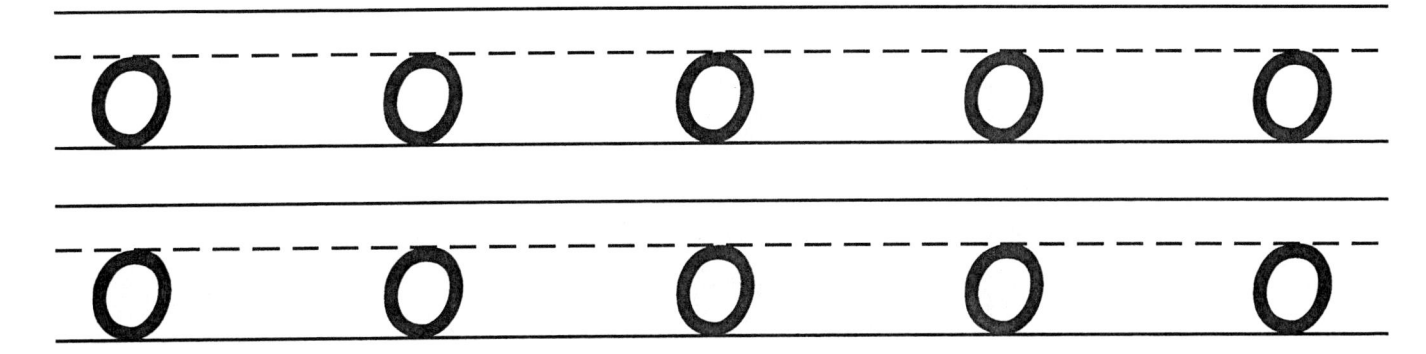

Ο   Ο   Ο   Ο   Ο

Ο   Ο   Ο   Ο   Ο

# More Practice with OMICRON

Omicron sounds like **o** in *obey*.

O     O     O     O     O

O     O     O     O     O

O     O     O     O     O

O     O     O     O     O

O     O     O     O     O

O     O     O     O     O

☐ I practiced my flashcards today.
(Remember to add this new card to your flashcards.)

# LET'S PRACTICE

Write fifteen letters of the Greek alphabet in order.

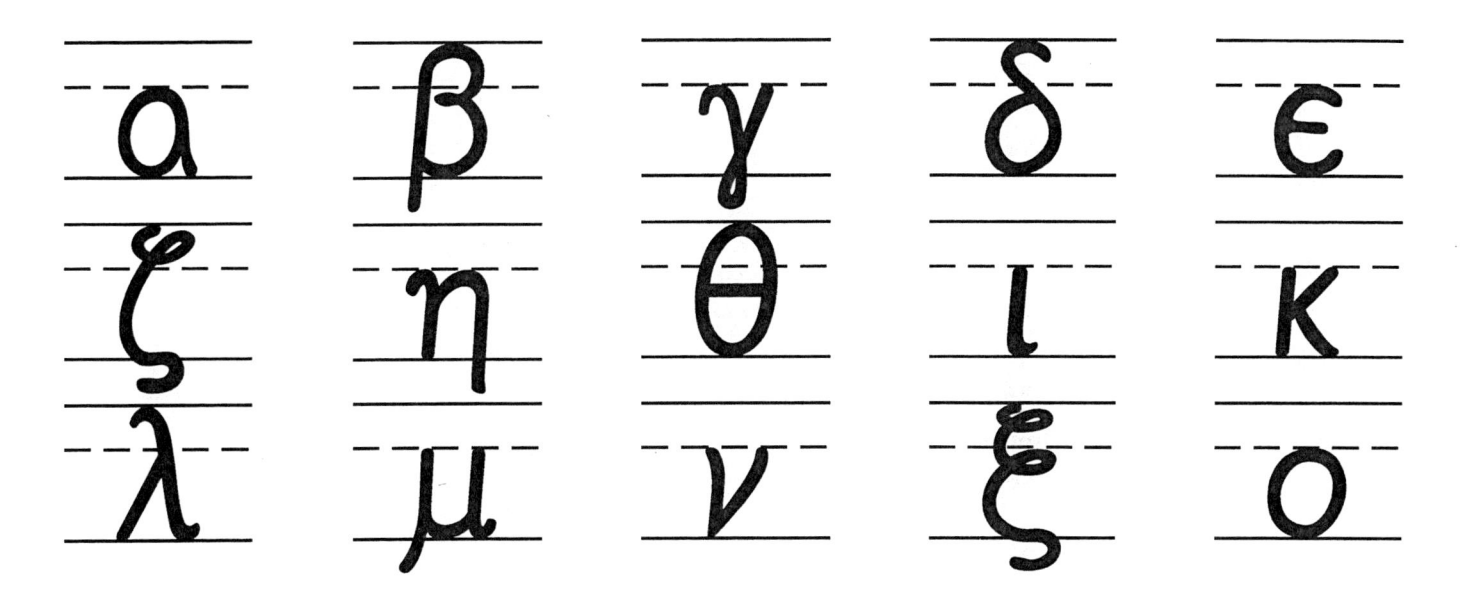

α  β  γ  δ  ε
ζ  η  θ  ι  κ
λ  μ  ν  ξ  ο

Circle the Greek letters that are the same in each box.

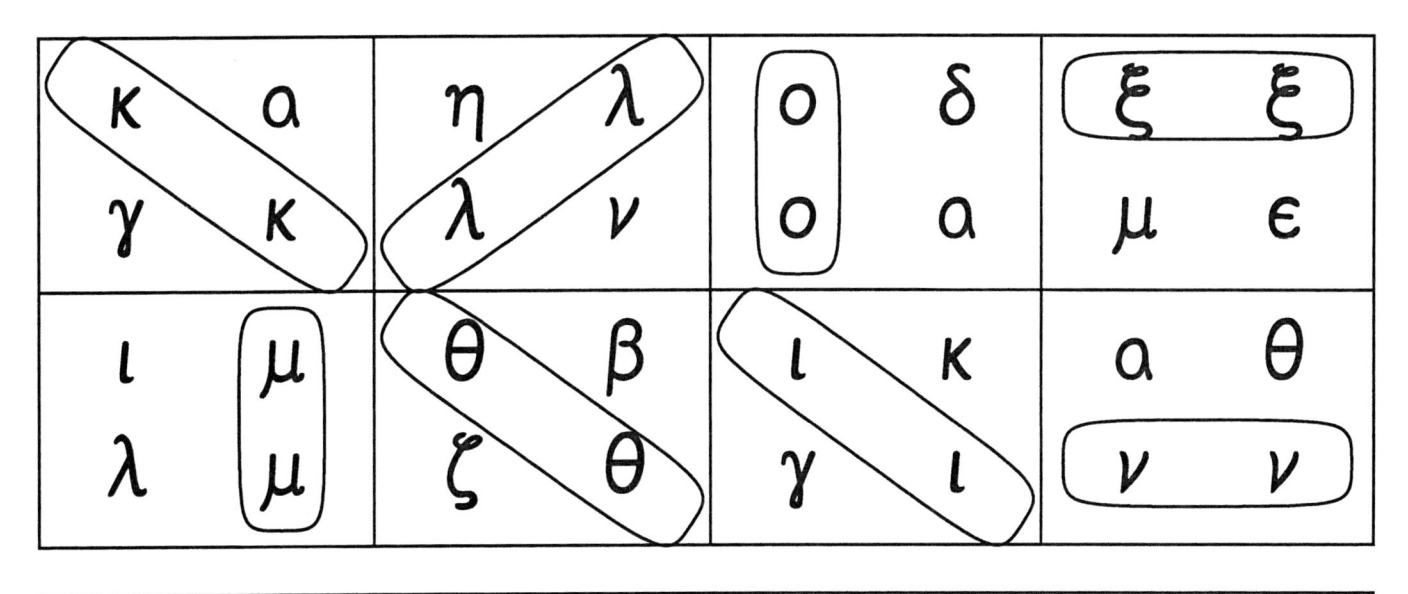

| κ  α  η  λ | ο  δ | ξ  ξ |
| γ  κ  λ  ν | ο  α | μ  ε |
| ι  μ  θ  β | ι  κ | α  θ |
| λ  μ  ζ  θ | γ  ι | ν  ν |

☐ I practiced my flashcards today.

# LET'S PRACTICE

Circle the correct letter names below the Greek letters.

| ν | ξ | β |
|---|---|---|
| kappa  (nu) | (xi)  nu | omicron  (beta) |
| κ | α | μ |
| theta  (kappa) | (alpha)  delta | (mu)  lambda |
| λ | ο | γ |
| iota  (lambda) | (omicron)  mu | (gamma)  xi |
| ι | ε | δ |
| eta  (iota) | (epsilon)  alpha | beta  (delta) |
| θ | η | ζ |
| zeta  (theta) | (eta)  epsilon | (zeta)  gamma |

☐ I practiced my flashcards today.

Lesson 16

# PI

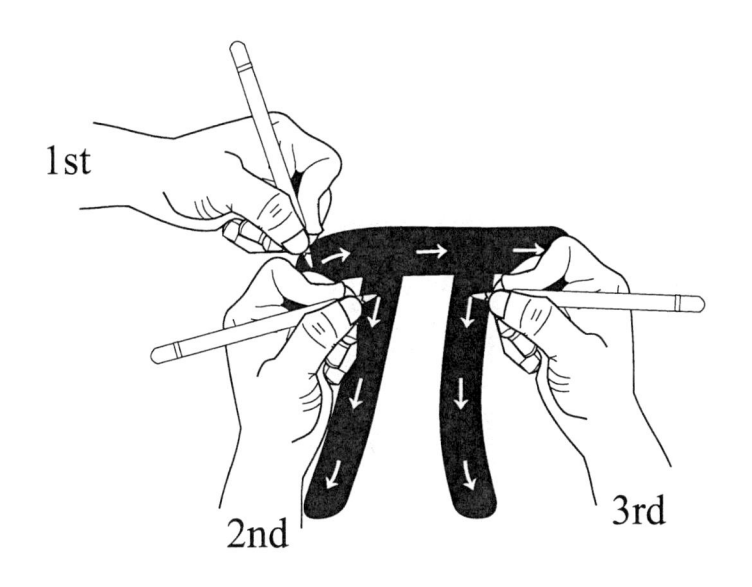

Write the letter *pi* across each line.
As you write it, say "**pie**."

# More Practice with PI

Pi sounds like **p** in *pie*.

π π π π π

π π π π π

π π π π π

π π π π π

π π π π π

π π π π π

☐ I practiced my flashcards today.
(Remember to add this new card to your flashcards.)

# LET'S PRACTICE

Write sixteen letters of the Greek alphabet in order.

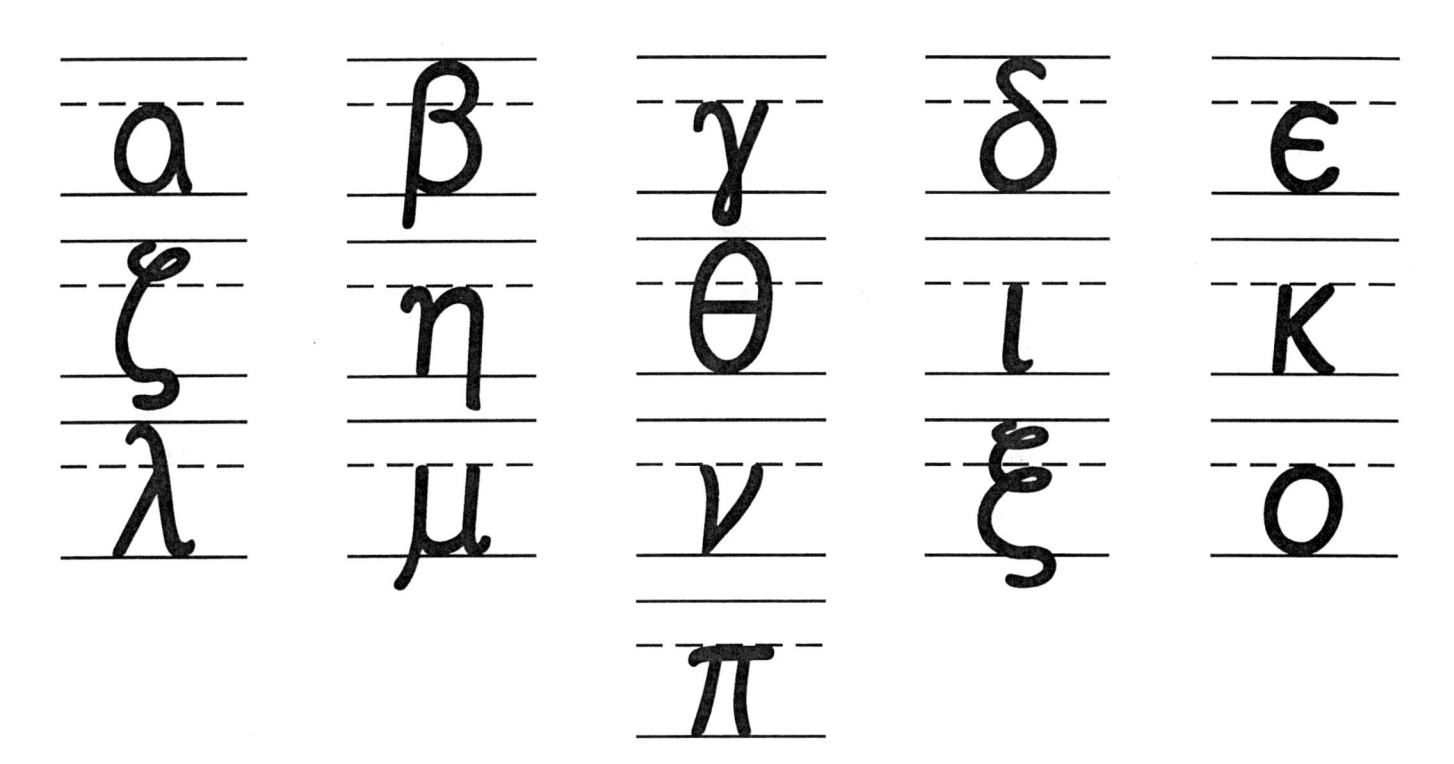

α  β  γ  δ  ε
ζ  η  θ  ι  κ
λ  μ  ν  ξ  ο
   π

Read the letter names in the big boxes. Circle all the Greek letters that belong to each name.

| pi | η | ⊡π | η | ⊡π | μ | ⊡π | ⊡π | ν | μ |
| omicron | ⊡ο | λ | ⊡ο | ⊡ο | θ | θ | ⊡ο | λ | θ |
| xi | ⊡ξ | ⊡ξ | κ | ⊡ξ | λ | ⊡ξ | κ | κ | λ |

☐ I practiced my flashcards today.

# LET'S PRACTICE

Draw lines from the Greek letters to their sounds.

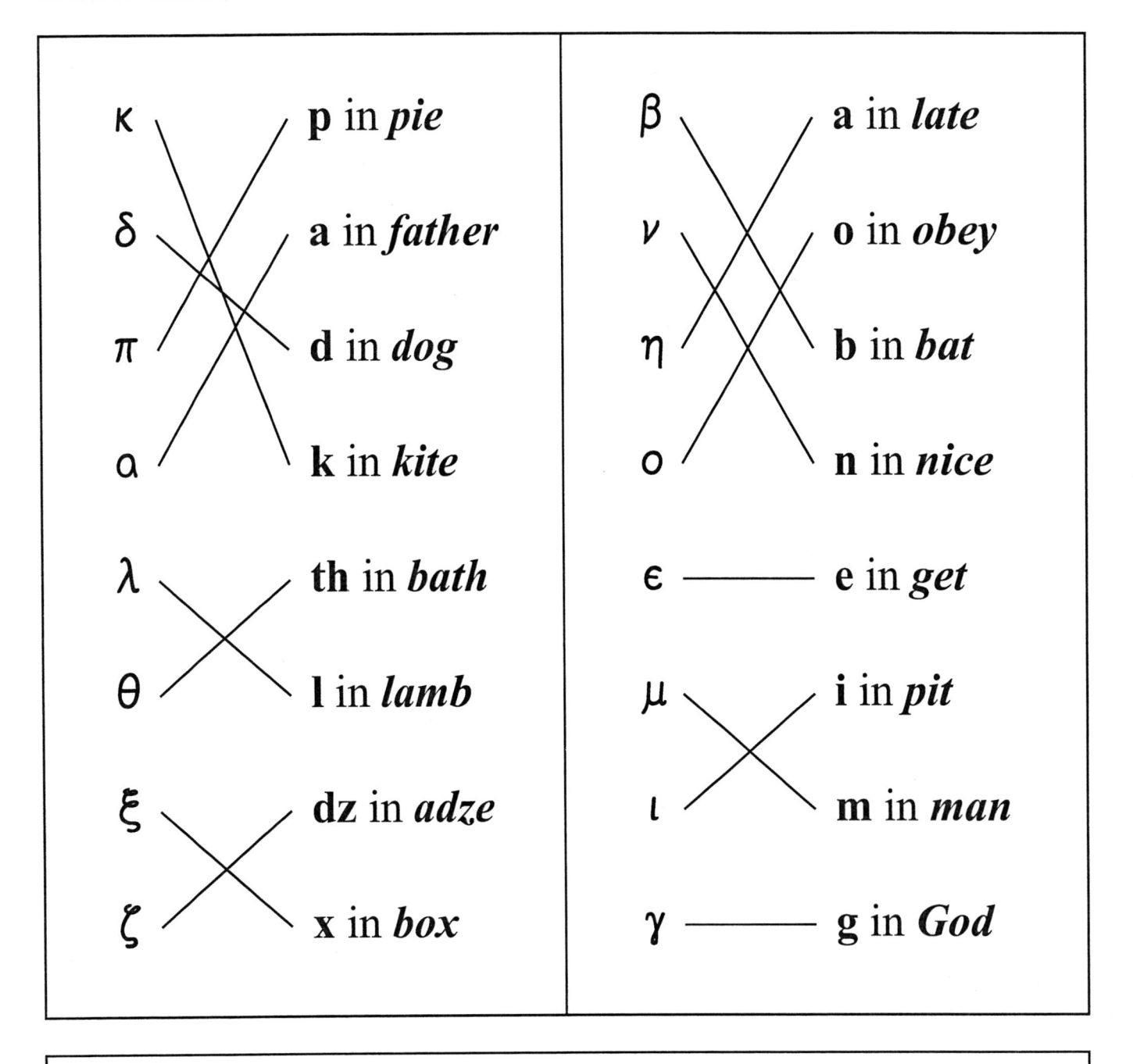

|  |  | |  |  |
|---|---|---|---|---|
| κ | k in *kite* | | β | b in *bat* |
| δ | d in *dog* | | ν | n in *nice* |
| π | p in *pie* | | η | a in *late* |
| α | a in *father* | | ο | o in *obey* |
| λ | l in *lamb* | | ε | e in *get* |
| θ | th in *bath* | | μ | m in *man* |
| ξ | x in *box* | | ι | i in *pit* |
| ζ | dz in *adze* | | γ | g in *God* |

☐ I practiced my flashcards today.

Lesson 17

# RHO

Write the letter *rho* across each line.
As you write it, say "**row**."

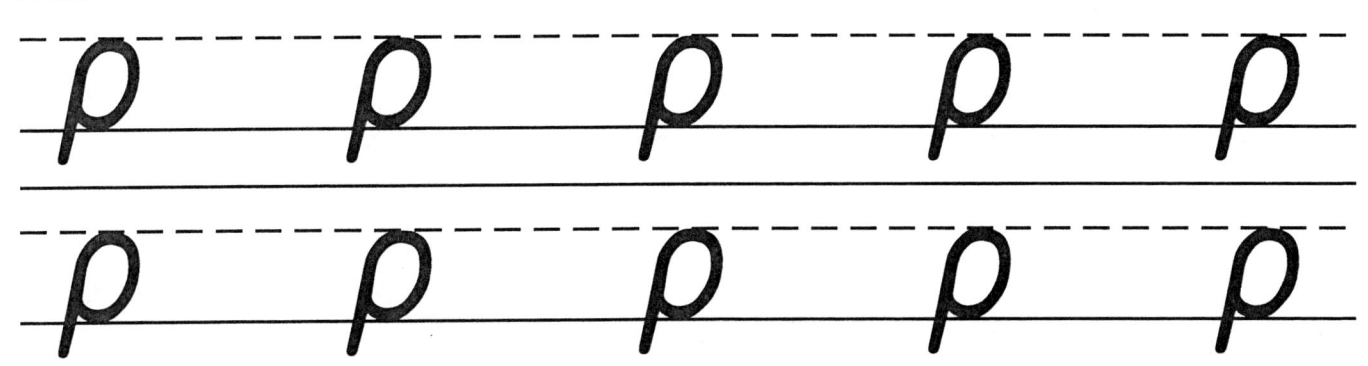

65

# More Practice with RHO

Rho sounds like **r** in *row*.

ρ ρ ρ ρ ρ

ρ ρ ρ ρ ρ

ρ ρ ρ ρ ρ

ρ ρ ρ ρ ρ

ρ ρ ρ ρ ρ

ρ ρ ρ ρ ρ

☐ I practiced my flashcards today.
(Remember to add this new card to your flashcards.)

# LET'S PRACTICE

Write seventeen letters of the Greek alphabet in order.

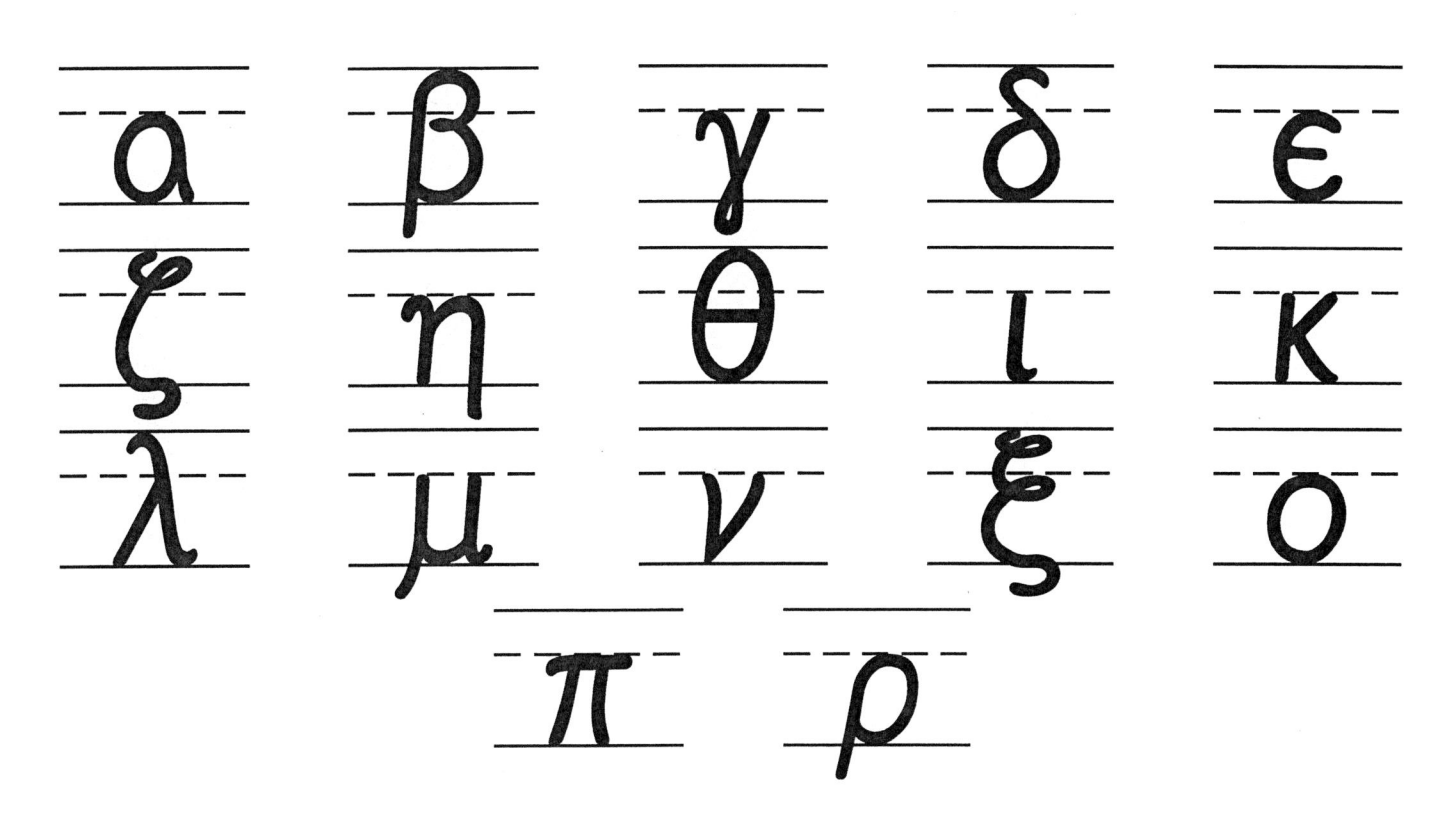

α   β   γ   δ   ε
ζ   η   θ   ι   κ
λ   μ   ν   ξ   ο
        π   ρ

What's my sound? Draw lines from the letters to the words that have that sound.

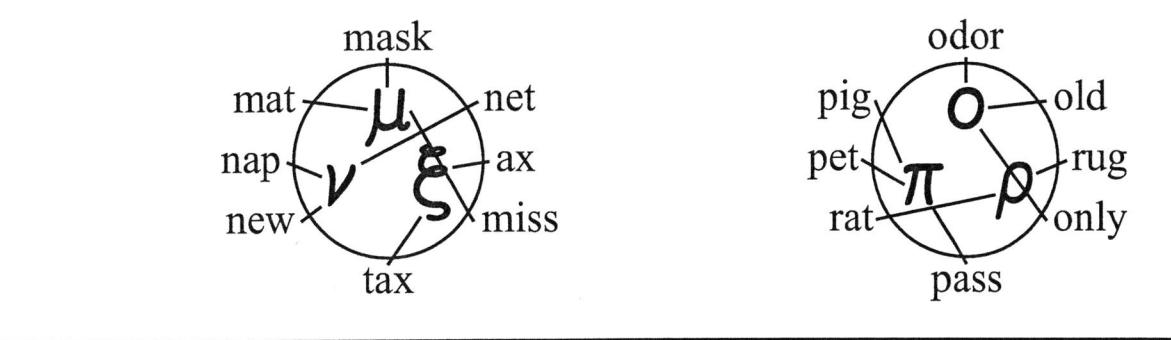

mask, mat, nap, new, tax, net, ax, miss — μ, ν, ξ, ζ

odor, pig, pet, rat, pass, old, rug, only — ο, π, ρ

☐ I practiced my flashcards today.

# LET'S PRACTICE

Write the names of the Greek letters.

α   alpha

β   beta

γ   gamma

δ   delta

ε   epsilon

ζ   zeta

η   eta

θ   theta

ι   iota

κ   kappa

λ   lambda

μ   mu

ν   nu

ξ   xi

ο   omicron

π   pi

ρ   rho

☐ I practiced my flashcards today.

Lesson 18

# SIGMA

(Both sigmas have the same sound. The σ is used at the beginning or middle of a word; the ς at the end.)

Write the letter *sigma* across each line.
As you write it, say "**sig**-ma."

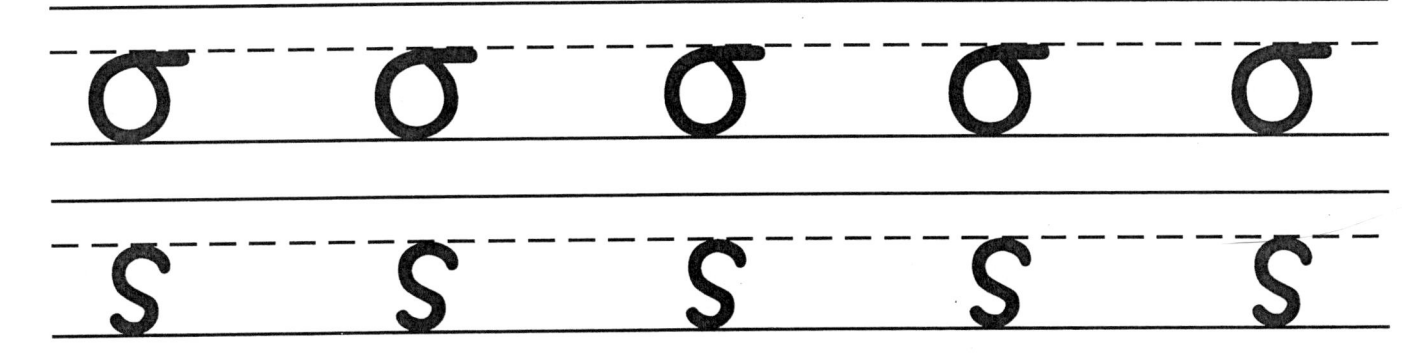

σ    σ    σ    σ    σ

ς    ς    ς    ς    ς

Greek Workbook - Level 1
Copyright © 1994 by Karen Mohs

# More Practice with SIGMA

## Sigma sounds like s in *sit*.

σ  σ  σ  σ  σ

ς  ς  ς  ς  ς

σ  σ  σ  σ  σ

ς  ς  ς  ς  ς

σ  σ  σ  σ  σ

ς  ς  ς  ς  ς

☐ I practiced my flashcards today.
(Remember to add these new cards to your flashcards.)

# LET'S PRACTICE

Write eighteen letters of the Greek alphabet in order.

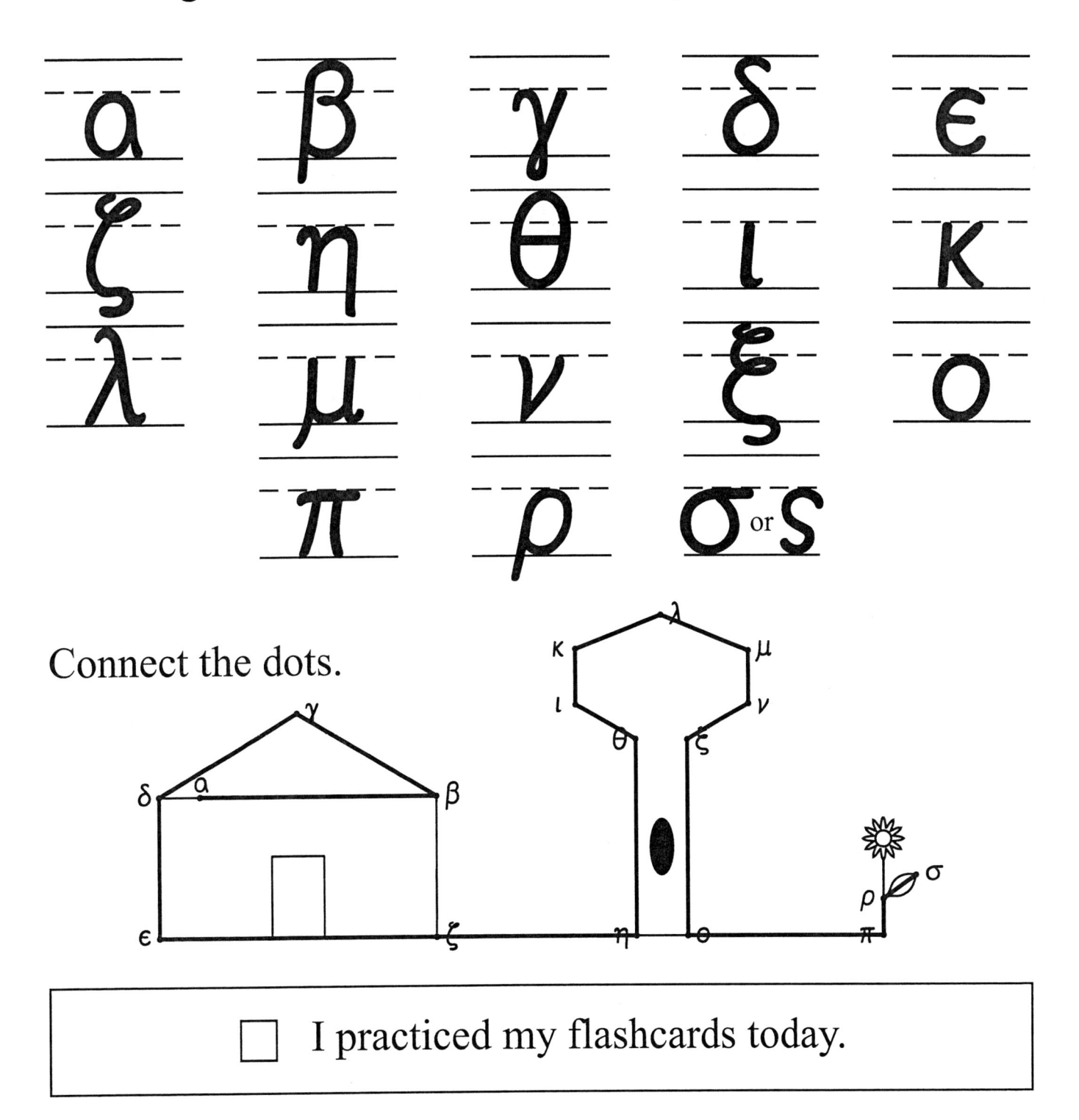

α    β    γ    δ    ε
ζ    η    θ    ι    κ
λ    μ    ν    ξ    ο
     π    ρ    σ or ς

Connect the dots.

☐ I practiced my flashcards today.

# LET'S PRACTICE

Draw lines from the Greek letters to their names.

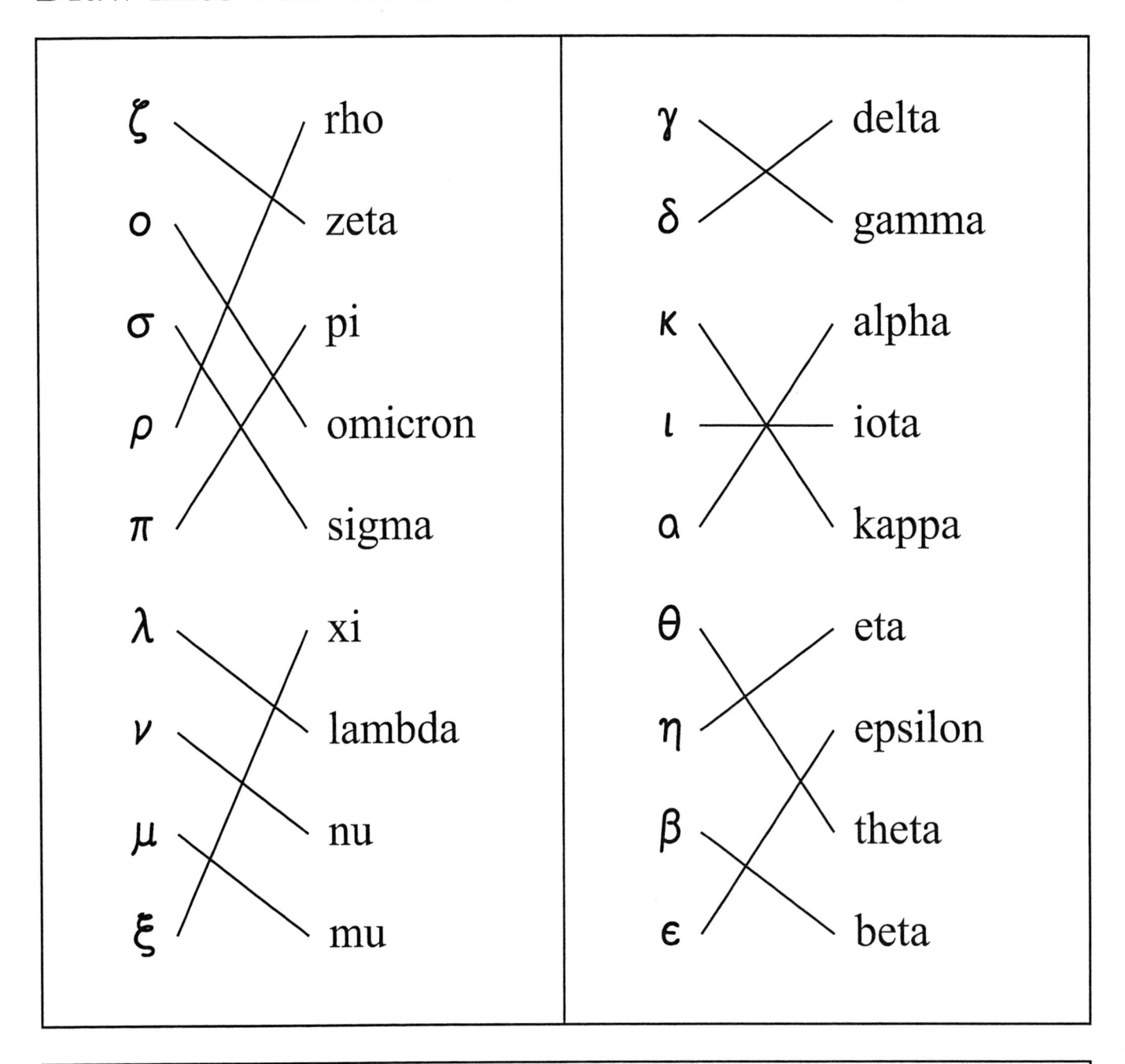

|  |  | |  |  |
|---|---|---|---|---|
| ζ | rho | | γ | delta |
| ο | zeta | | δ | gamma |
| σ | pi | | κ | alpha |
| ρ | omicron | | ι | iota |
| π | sigma | | α | kappa |
| λ | xi | | θ | eta |
| ν | lambda | | η | epsilon |
| μ | nu | | β | theta |
| ξ | mu | | ε | beta |

☐ I practiced my flashcards today.

Lesson 19

# TAU

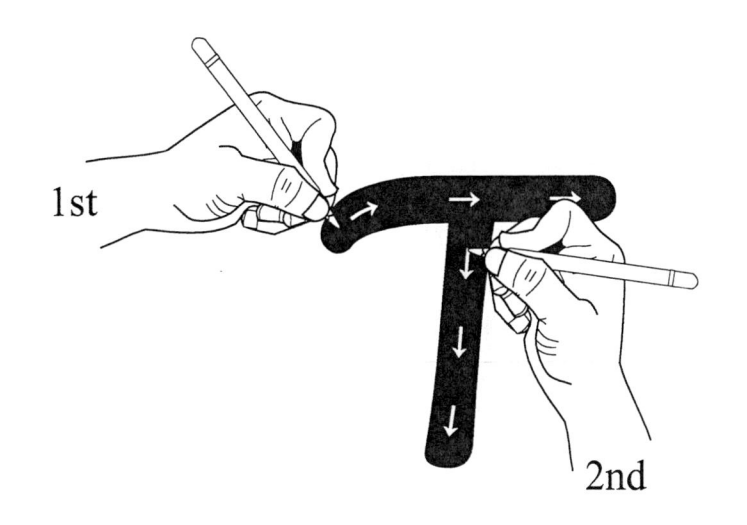

Write the letter *tau* across each line.
As you write it, say **"tou."**

Greek Workbook - Level 1
Copyright © 1994 by Karen Mohs

73

# More Practice with TAU

Tau sounds like **t** in *toy*.

☐ I practiced my flashcards today.
(Remember to add this new card to your flashcards.)

# LET'S PRACTICE

Write nineteen letters of the Greek alphabet in order.

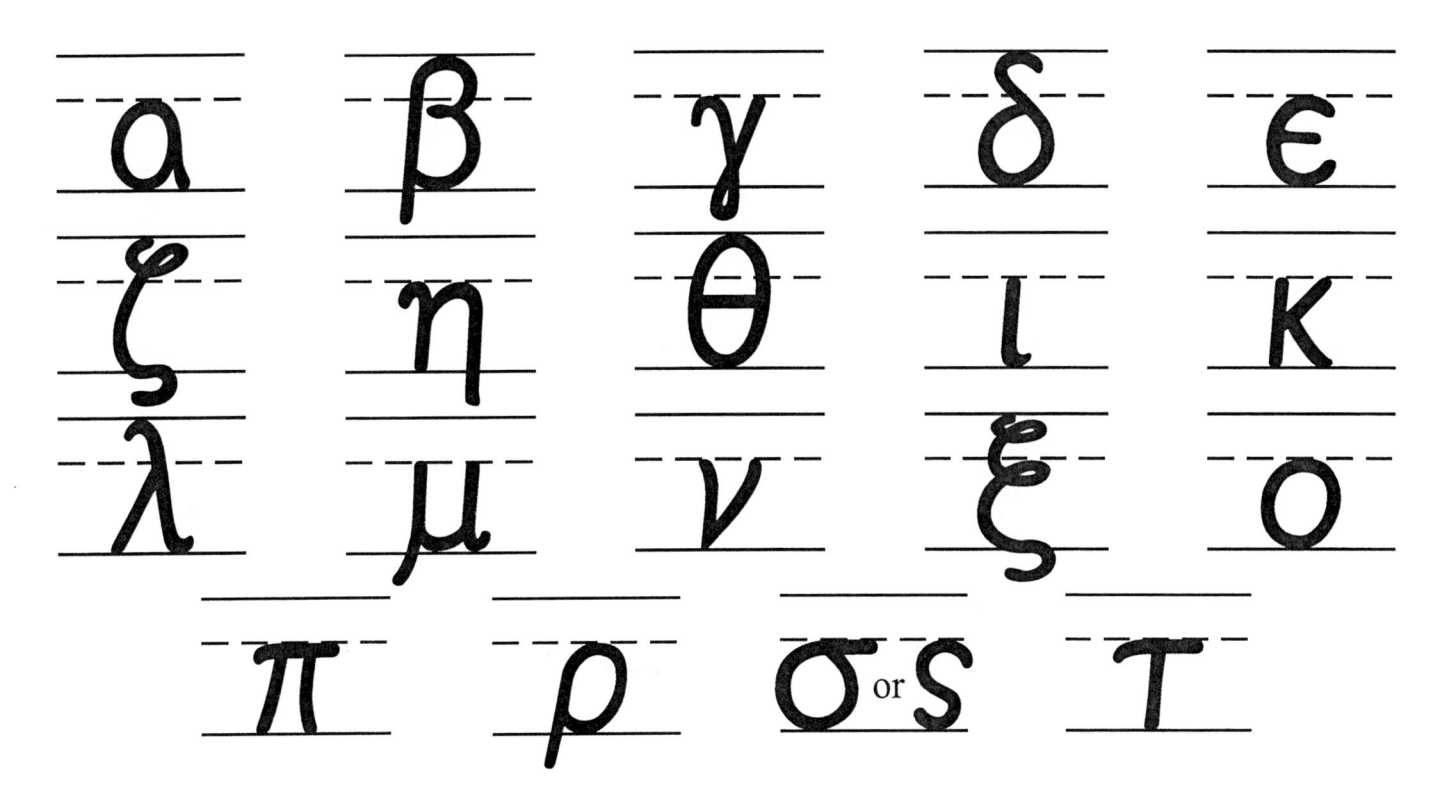

α  β  γ  δ  ε
ζ  η  θ  ι  κ
λ  μ  ν  ξ  ο
π  ρ  σ or ς  τ

Look at the Greek letter at the top of each box. Find that letter in the words below and circle it.

| π | ρ | σ | τ |
|---|---|---|---|
| πέπωκε<br>πέριξ<br>πέντε | ῥίπτω<br>ῥήγνυμι<br>ῥαντίζω | σινδών<br>σκηνήν<br>στάσιν | τρίτη<br>τίκτω<br>ταῦτα |

☐ I practiced my flashcards today.

# LET'S PRACTICE

Draw circles around the Greek letters and their names.

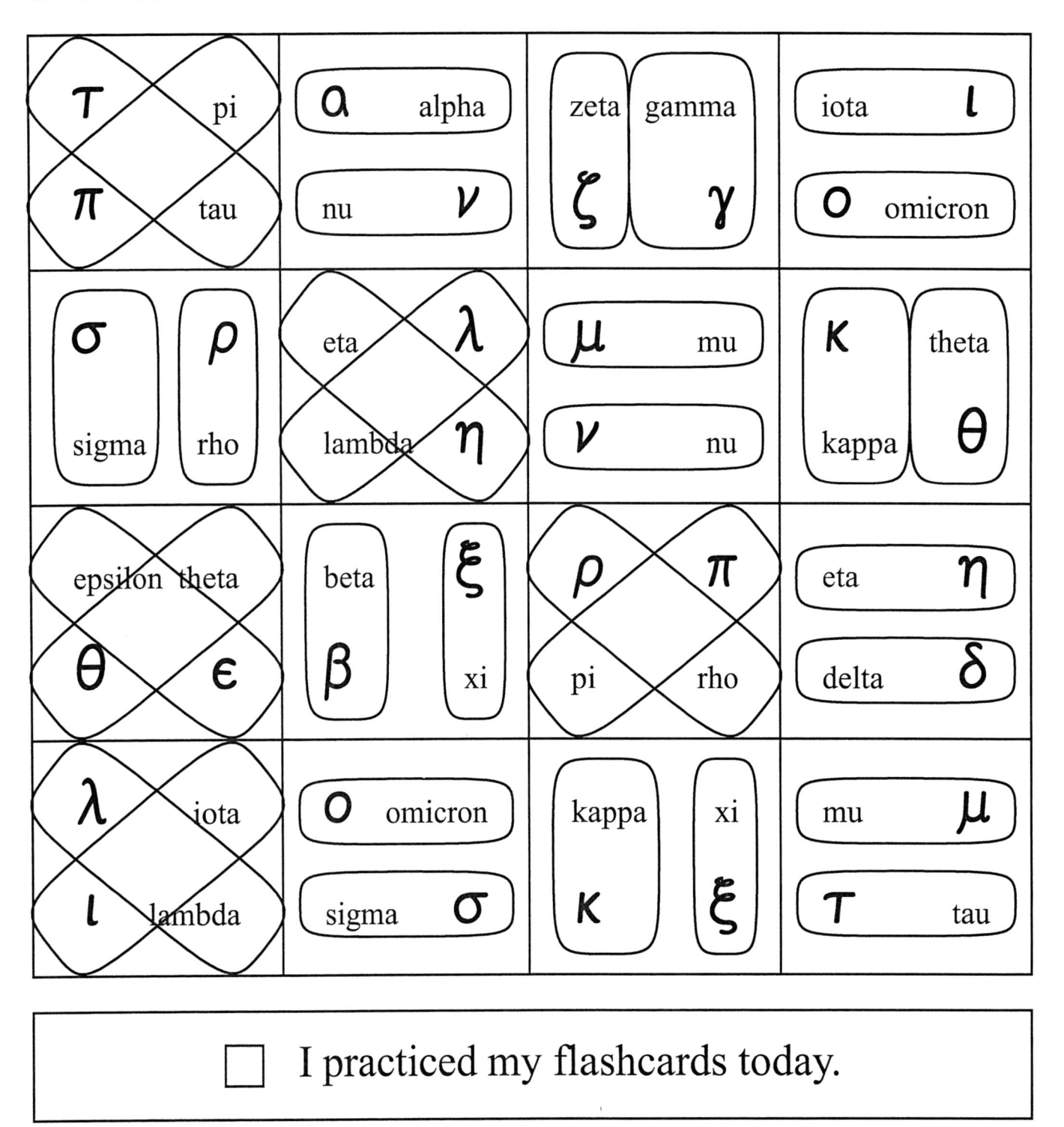

| | | | |
|---|---|---|---|
| τ pi / π tau | α alpha / nu ν | zeta gamma / ζ γ | iota ι / ο omicron |
| σ ρ / sigma rho | eta λ / lambda η | μ mu / ν nu | κ theta / kappa θ |
| epsilon theta / θ ε | beta ξ / β xi | ρ π / pi rho | eta η / delta δ |
| λ iota / ι lambda | ο omicron / sigma σ | kappa xi / κ ξ | mu μ / τ tau |

☐ I practiced my flashcards today.

Lesson 20

# UPSILON

Write the letter *upsilon* across each line.
As you write it, say "**up**-si-lon."

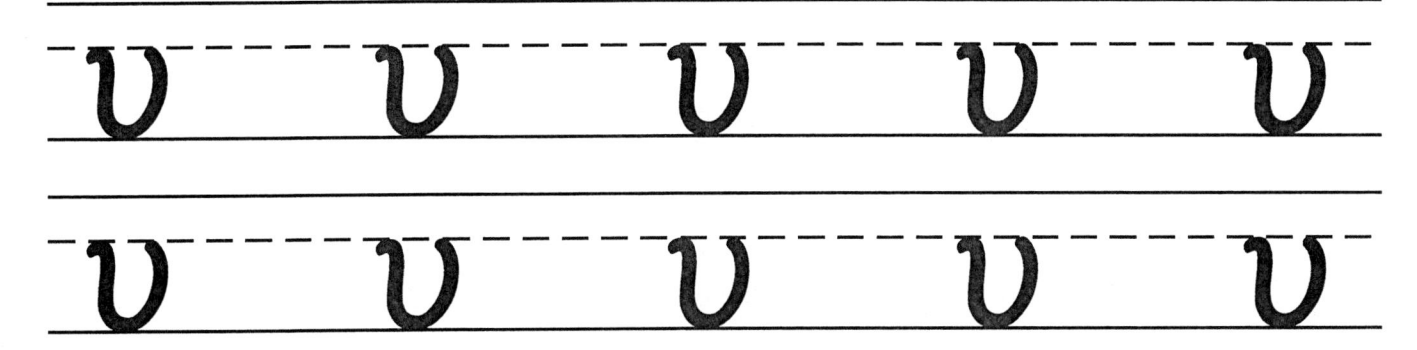

υ  υ  υ  υ  υ

υ  υ  υ  υ  υ

# More Practice with UPSILON

Upsilon sounds like **oo** in *good*.

υ　　υ　　υ　　υ　　υ

υ　　υ　　υ　　υ　　υ

υ　　υ　　υ　　υ　　υ

υ　　υ　　υ　　υ　　υ

υ　　υ　　υ　　υ　　υ

υ　　υ　　υ　　υ　　υ

☐ I practiced my flashcards today.
(Remember to add this new card to your flashcards.)

# LET'S PRACTICE

Write twenty letters of the Greek alphabet in order.

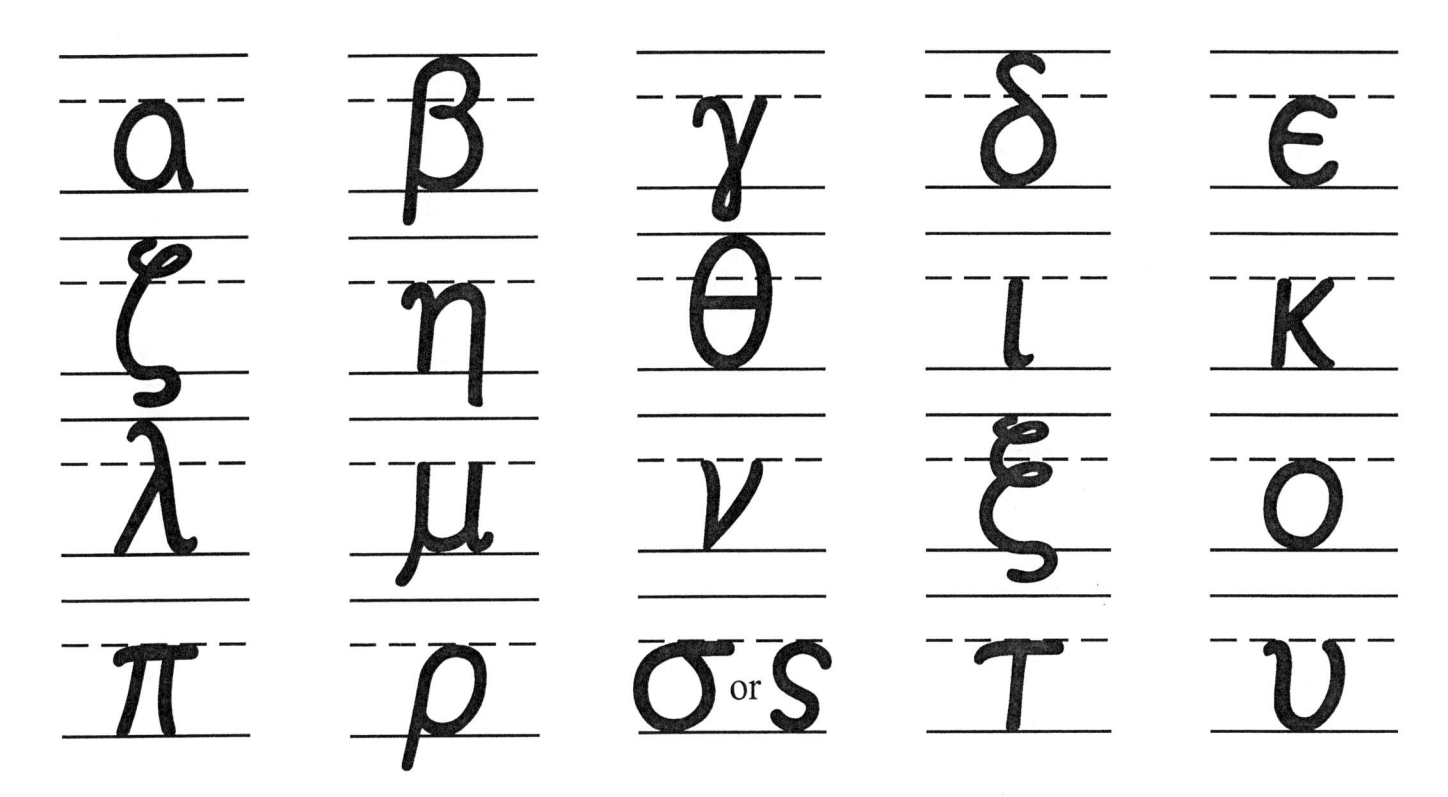

| α | β | γ | δ | ε |
| ζ | η | θ | ι | κ |
| λ | μ | ν | ξ | ο |
| π | ρ | σ or ς | τ | υ |

Color the boxes orange if the letters match the letter in the larger box at the beginning of each row.

| | | | | | | | | | | |
|---|---|---|---|---|---|---|---|---|---|---|
| τ | π | λ | κ | **τ** | κ | π | **τ** | μ | **τ** | λ |
|   | **τ** | π | μ | λ | π | μ | λ | π | **τ** | κ |
| υ | **υ** | γ | **υ** | ν | γ | **υ** | σ | η | ο | ν |
|   | ν | η | **υ** | σ | ν | η | ο | **υ** | γ | η |

☐ I practiced my flashcards today.

# LET'S PRACTICE

Circle the name of the Greek letter at the beginning of each row.

| ξ | alpha | mu | lambda | delta |
|---|---|---|---|---|
|   | epsilon | zeta | (xi) | pi |
| σ | delta | (sigma) | eta | nu |
|   | iota | gamma | omicron | theta |
| υ | zeta | rho | theta | (upsilon) |
|   | epsilon | lambda | tau | sigma |
| π | iota | xi | beta | nu |
|   | (pi) | zeta | mu | kappa |
| τ | kappa | (tau) | theta | iota |
|   | alpha | sigma | eta | delta |
| o | delta | gamma | theta | upsilon |
|   | alpha | iota | mu | (omicron) |
| ρ | (rho) | beta | pi | delta |
|   | tau | theta | gamma | lambda |

☐ I practiced my flashcards today.

Lesson 21

# PHI

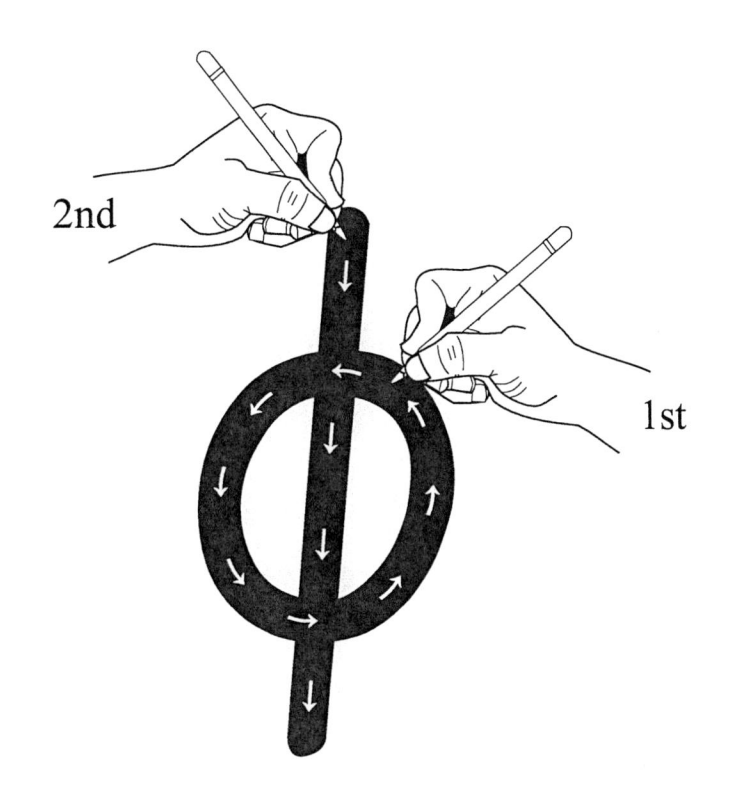

Write the letter *phi* across each line.
As you write it, say "**fee**."

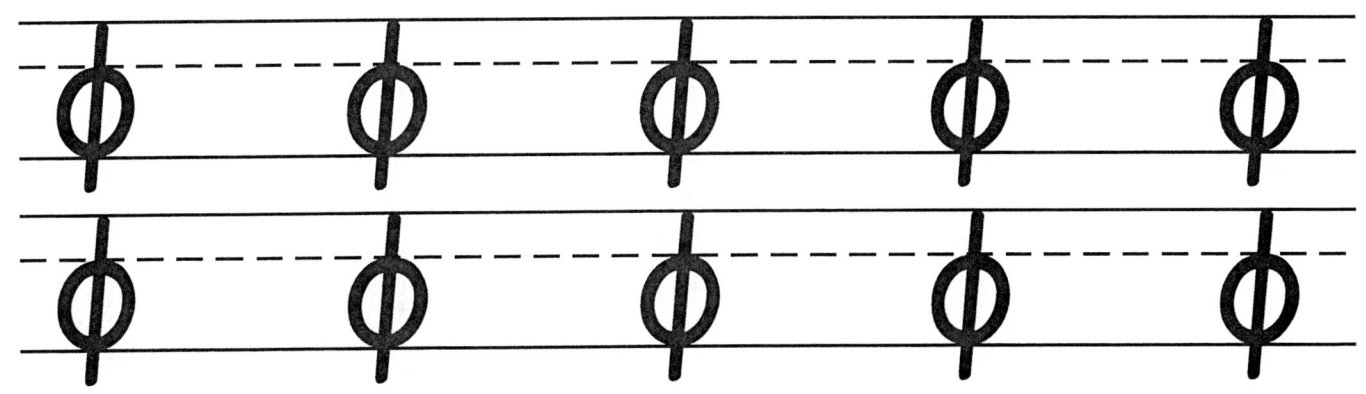

# More Practice with PHI

*Phi sounds like **f** in *fun*.*

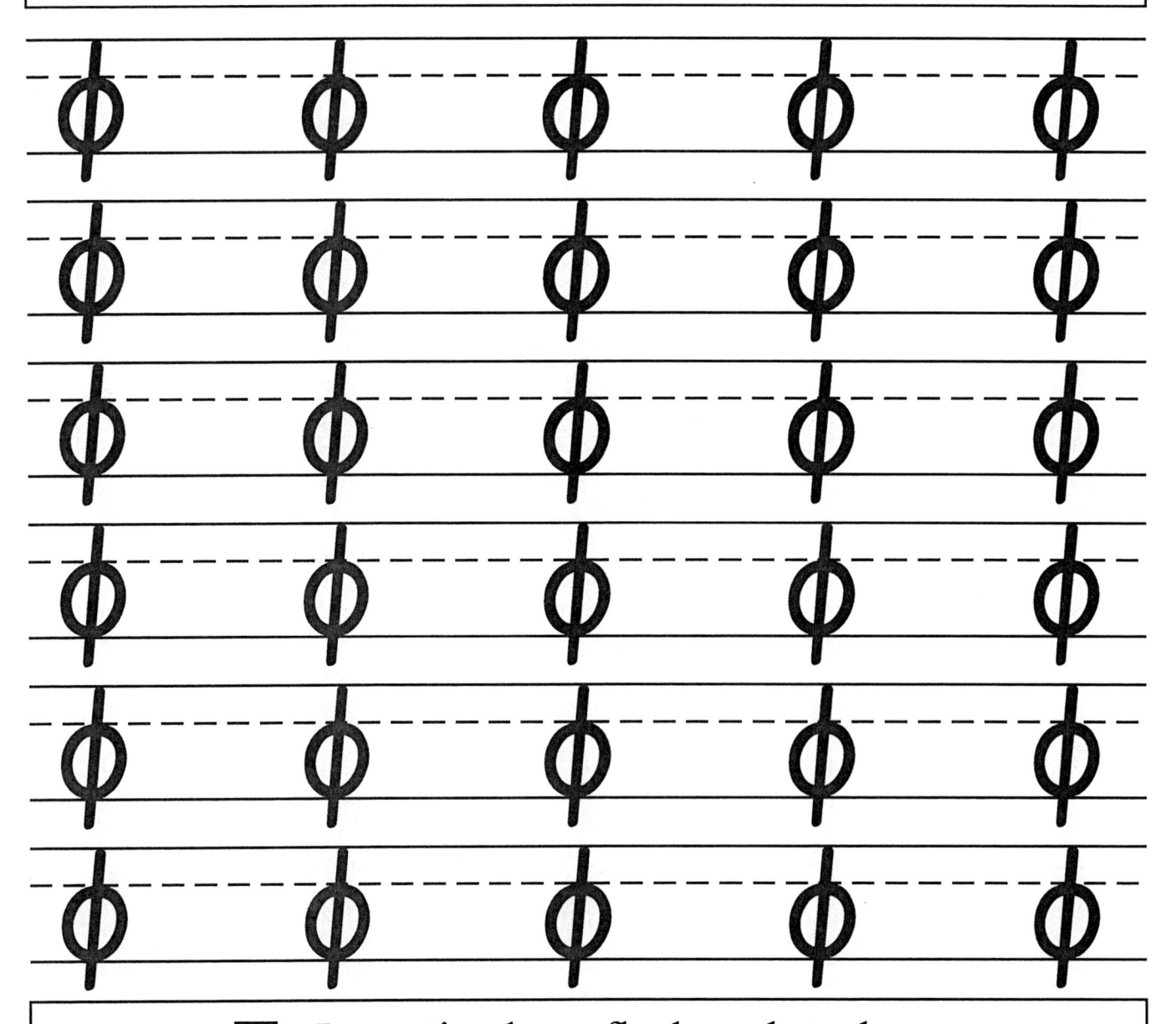

φ  φ  φ  φ  φ

φ  φ  φ  φ  φ

φ  φ  φ  φ  φ

φ  φ  φ  φ  φ

φ  φ  φ  φ  φ

φ  φ  φ  φ  φ

☐ I practiced my flashcards today.
(Remember to add this new card to your flashcards.)

# LET'S PRACTICE

Write twenty-one letters of the Greek alphabet in order.

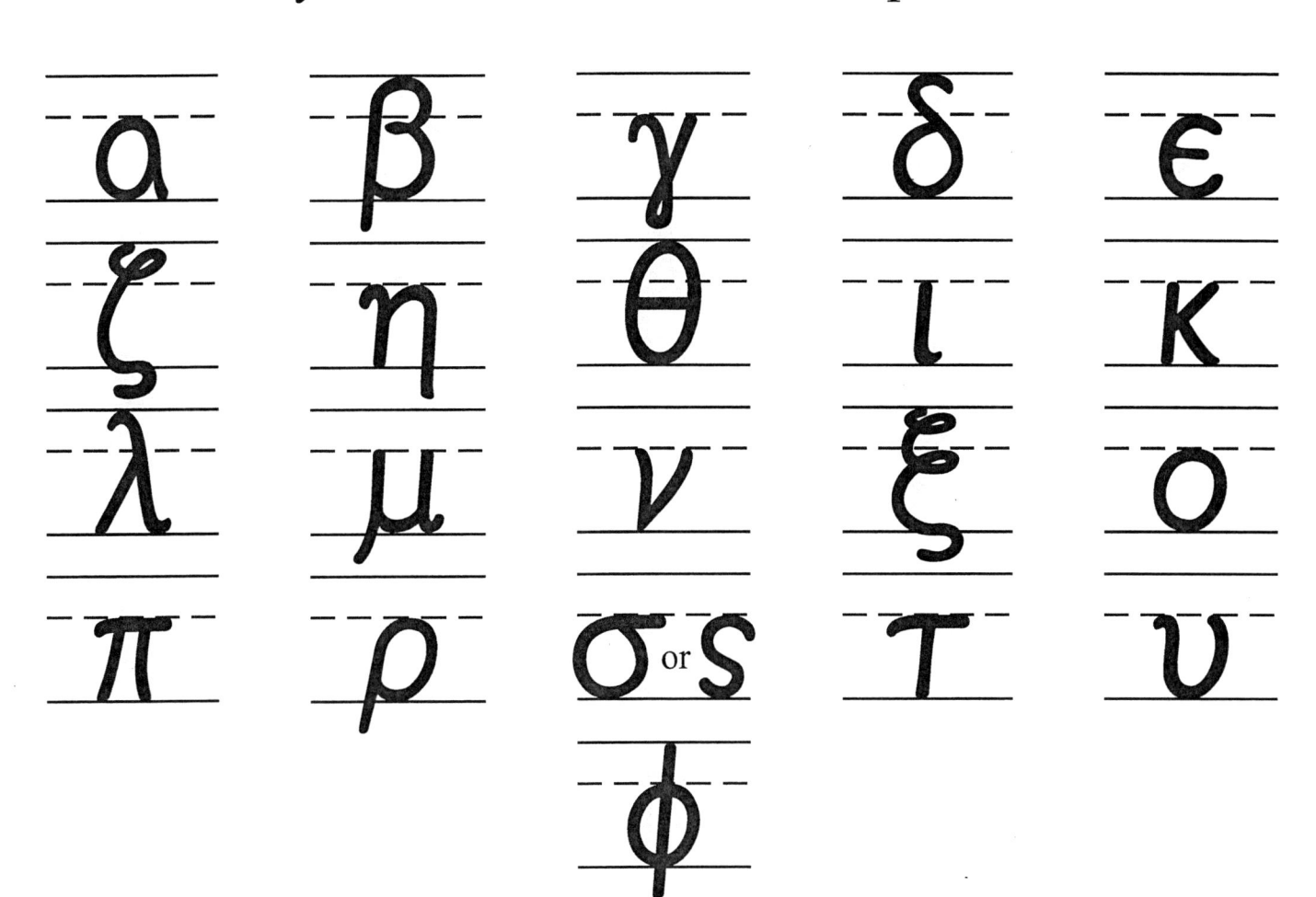

| α | β | γ | δ | ε |
| ζ | η | θ | ι | κ |
| λ | μ | ν | ξ | ο |
| π | ρ | σ or ς | τ | υ |
|   |   | φ |   |   |

Circle the words that have the Greek letter sound.

| φ | (fun) | (face) | bug |
|---|---|---|---|
|   | one | (fish) | game |

☐ I practiced my flashcards today.

# LET'S PRACTICE

Draw stems on the flowers to put them in their own vases.

Vases: xi, omicron, pi, rho, sigma, tau, upsilon, phi

☐ I practiced my flashcards today.

Lesson 22

# CHI

Write the letter *chi* across each line.
As you write it, say **"kee."**

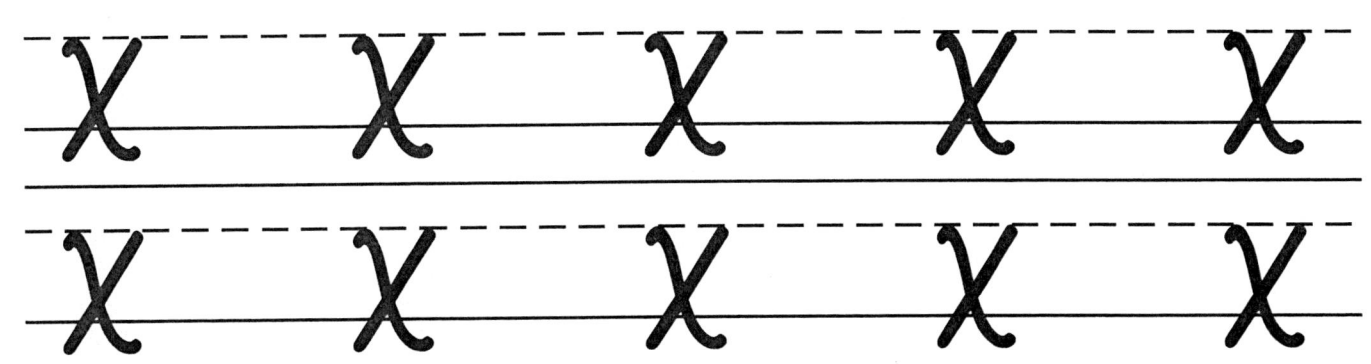

Greek Workbook - Level 1
Copyright © 1994 by Karen Mohs

# More Practice with CHI

Chi sounds like the German **ch** in *Ach*.

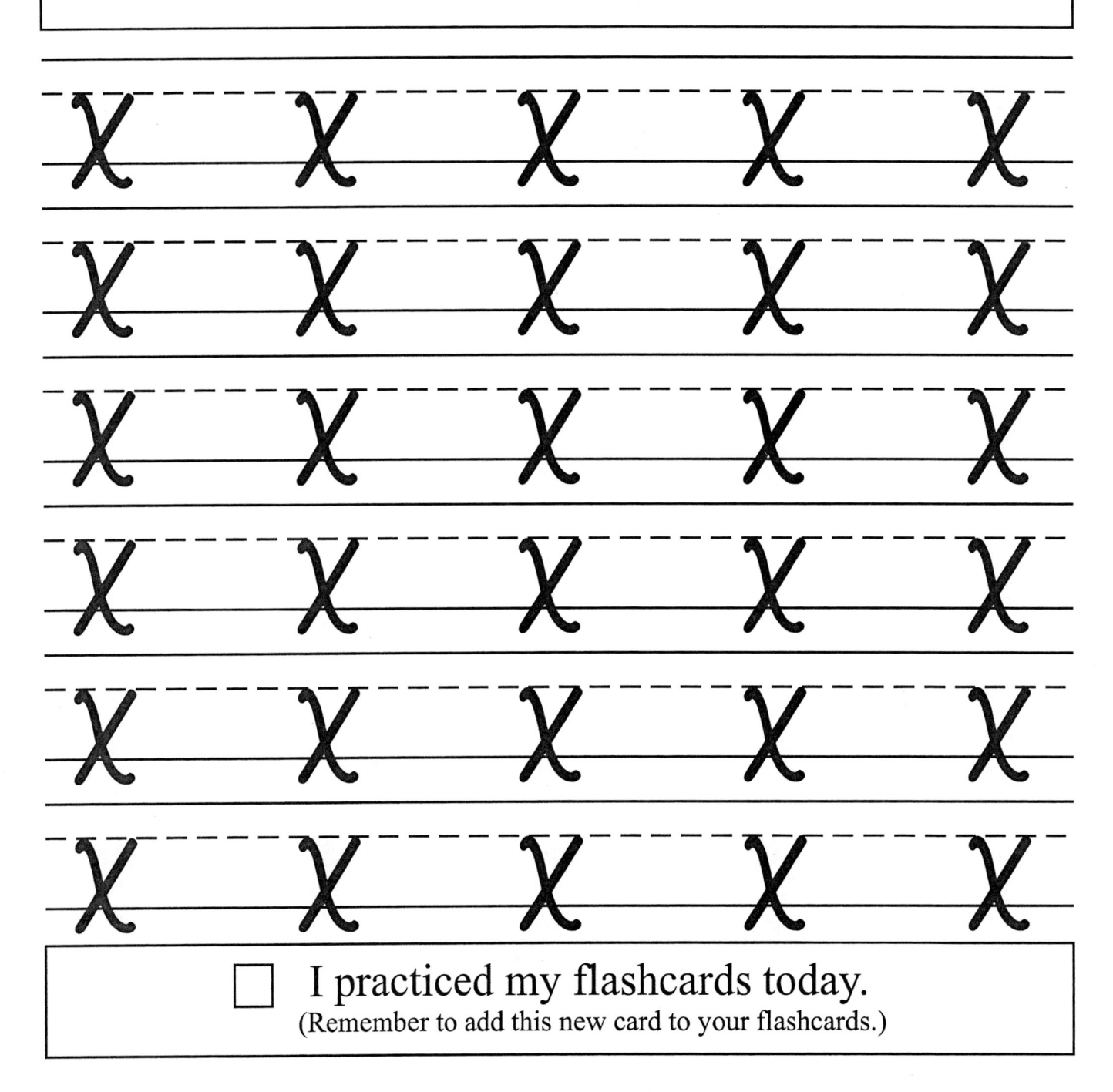

χ χ χ χ χ

χ χ χ χ χ

χ χ χ χ χ

χ χ χ χ χ

χ χ χ χ χ

χ χ χ χ χ

☐ I practiced my flashcards today.
(Remember to add this new card to your flashcards.)

# LET'S PRACTICE

Write twenty-two letters of the Greek alphabet in order.

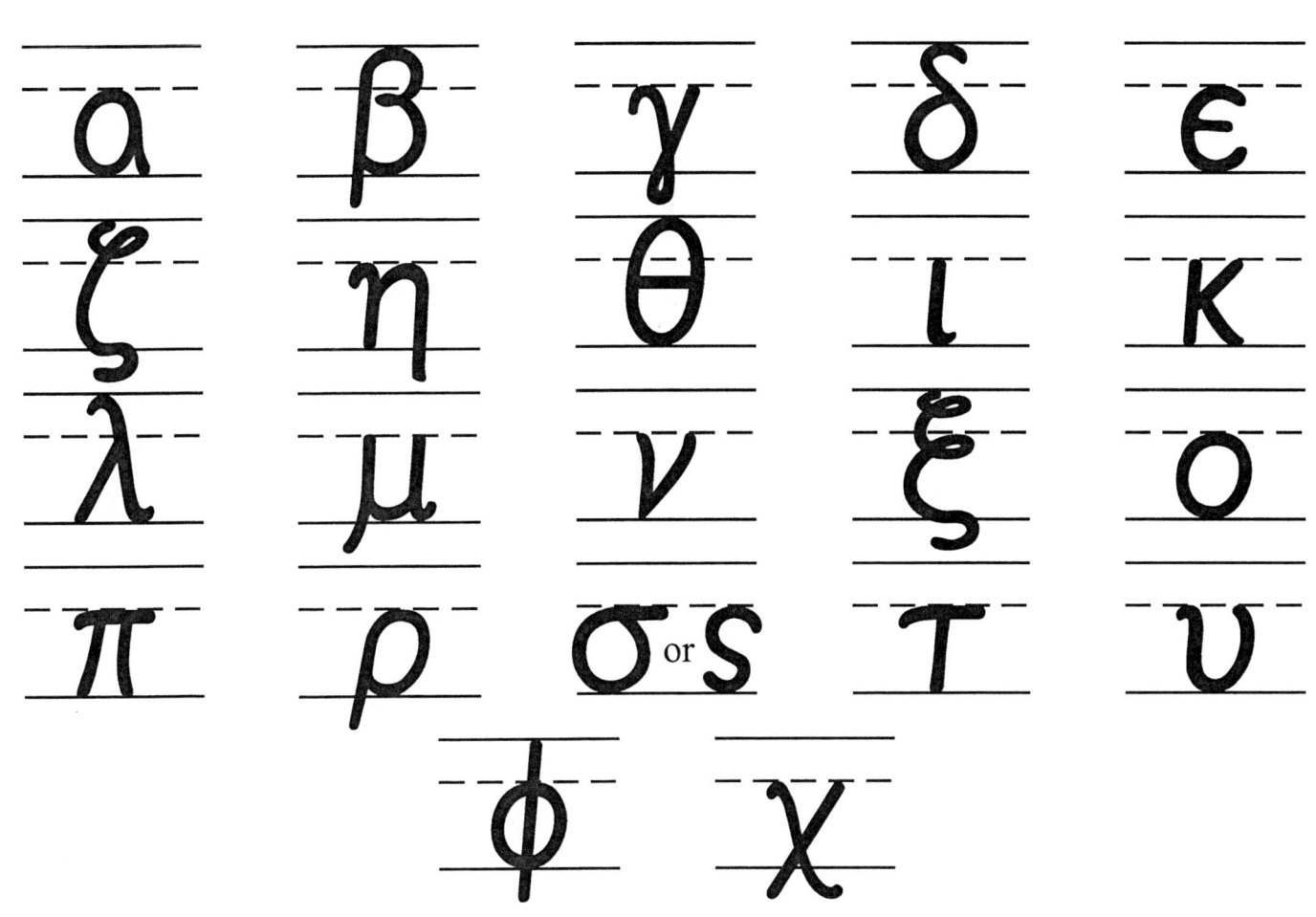

| α | β | γ | δ | ε |
| ζ | η | θ | ι | κ |
| λ | μ | ν | ξ | ο |
| π | ρ | σ or ς | τ | υ |
|   |   | φ | χ |   |

Draw lines through three Greek letters that are alike.

| ~~χ~~ ~~χ~~ ~~χ~~<br>φ ρ φ | υ ο ο<br>~~σ~~ ~~σ~~ ~~σ~~ | π π τ<br>~~τ~~ ~~τ~~ ~~τ~~ | ~~ξ~~ ~~ξ~~ ~~ξ~~<br>χ φ χ |

☐ I practiced my flashcards today.

# LET'S PRACTICE

Color the triangle if the letter name matches the Greek letter at the top.

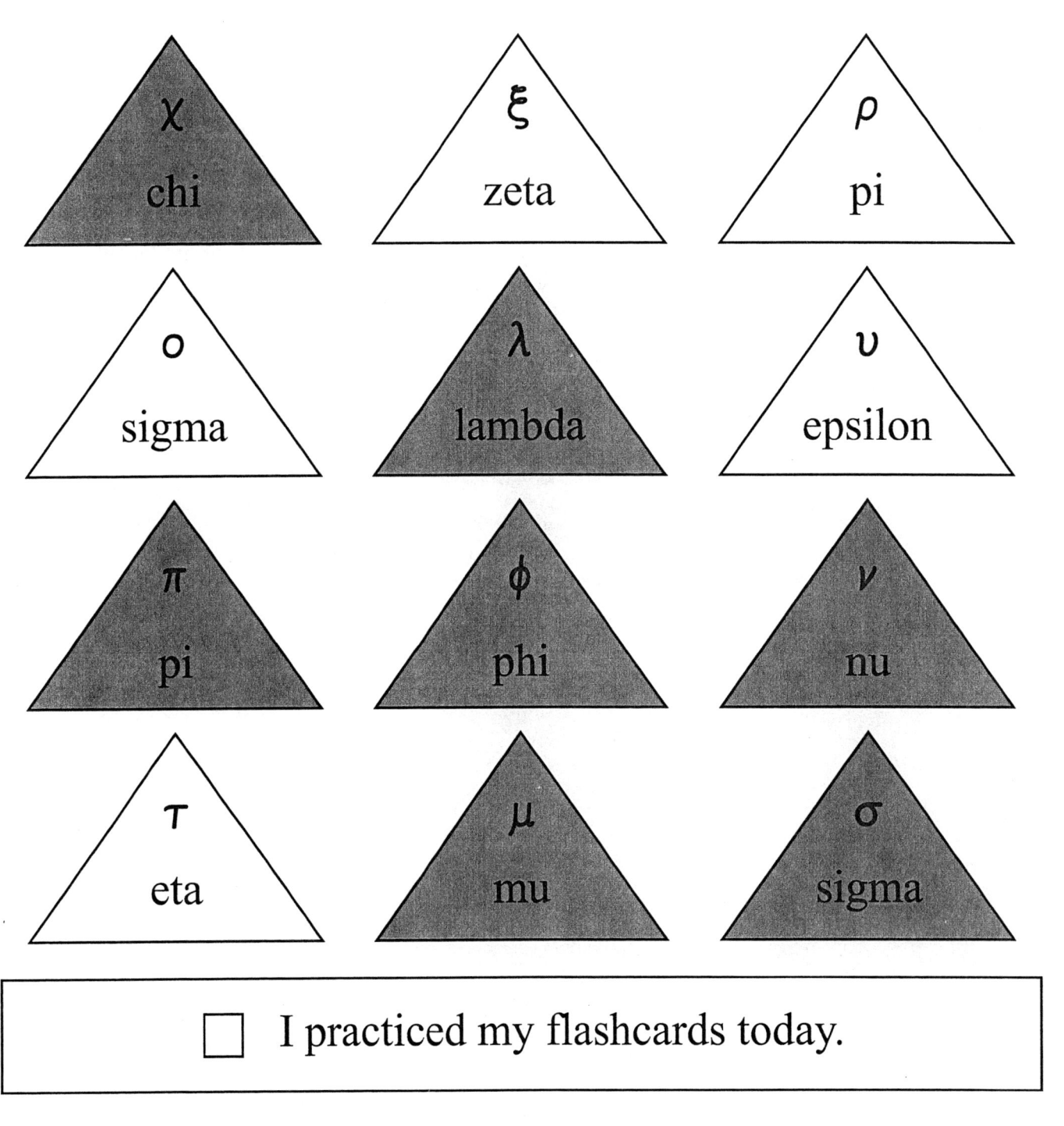

| Greek letter | Name | Match? |
|---|---|---|
| χ | chi | ✓ (colored) |
| ξ | zeta | ✗ |
| ρ | pi | ✗ |
| ο | sigma | ✗ |
| λ | lambda | ✓ (colored) |
| υ | epsilon | ✗ |
| π | pi | ✓ (colored) |
| φ | phi | ✓ (colored) |
| ν | nu | ✓ (colored) |
| τ | eta | ✗ |
| μ | mu | ✓ (colored) |
| σ | sigma | ✓ (colored) |

☐ I practiced my flashcards today.

Lesson 23

# PSI

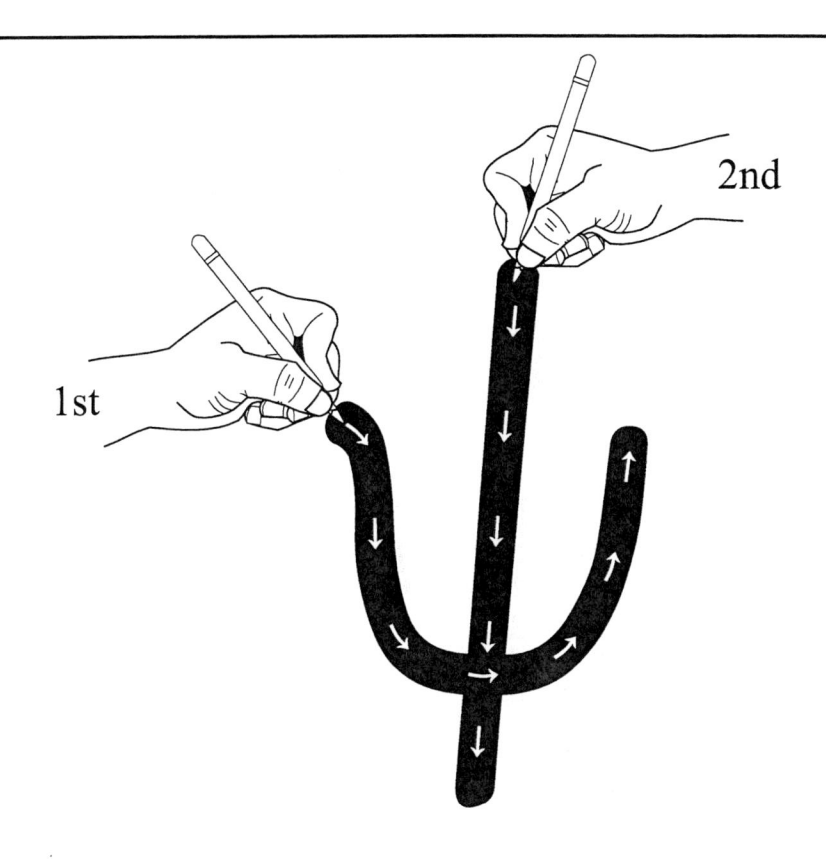

Write the letter *psi* across each line.
As you write it, say "**psee**."

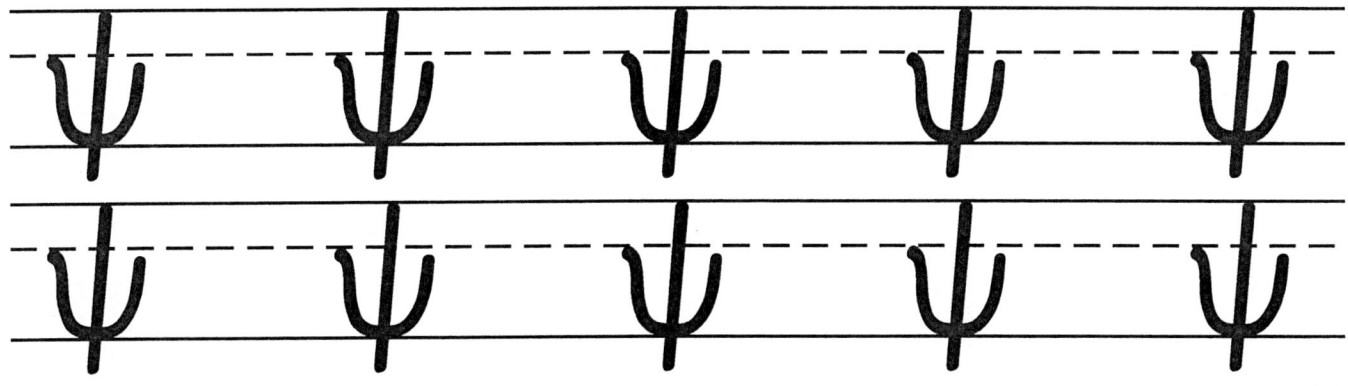

Greek Workbook - Level 1
Copyright © 1994 by Karen Mohs

# More Practice with PSI

Psi sounds like **ps** in *lips*.

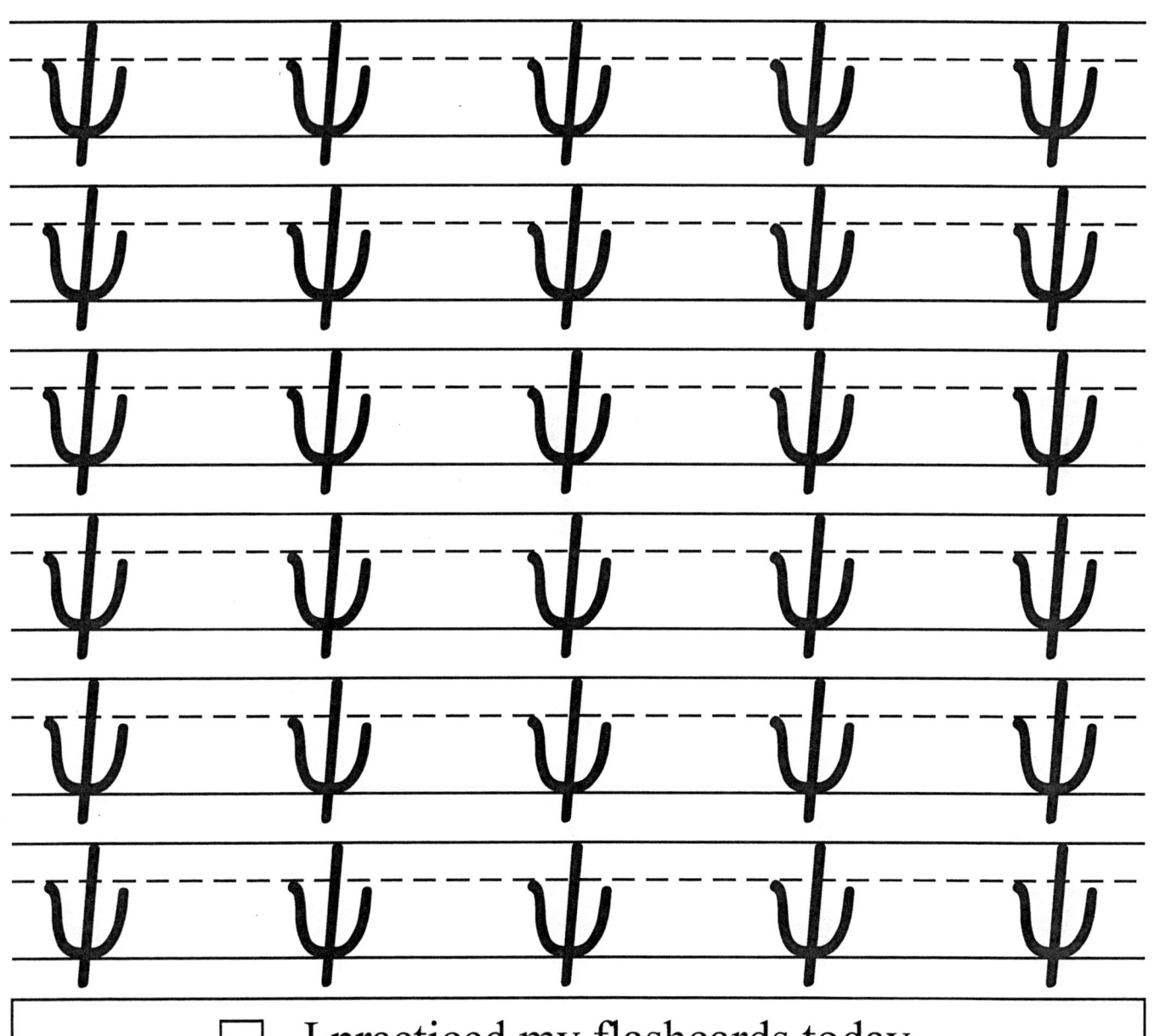

ψ ψ ψ ψ ψ
ψ ψ ψ ψ ψ
ψ ψ ψ ψ ψ
ψ ψ ψ ψ ψ
ψ ψ ψ ψ ψ
ψ ψ ψ ψ ψ

☐ I practiced my flashcards today.
(Remember to add this new card to your flashcards.)

# LET'S PRACTICE

Write twenty-three letters of the Greek alphabet in order.

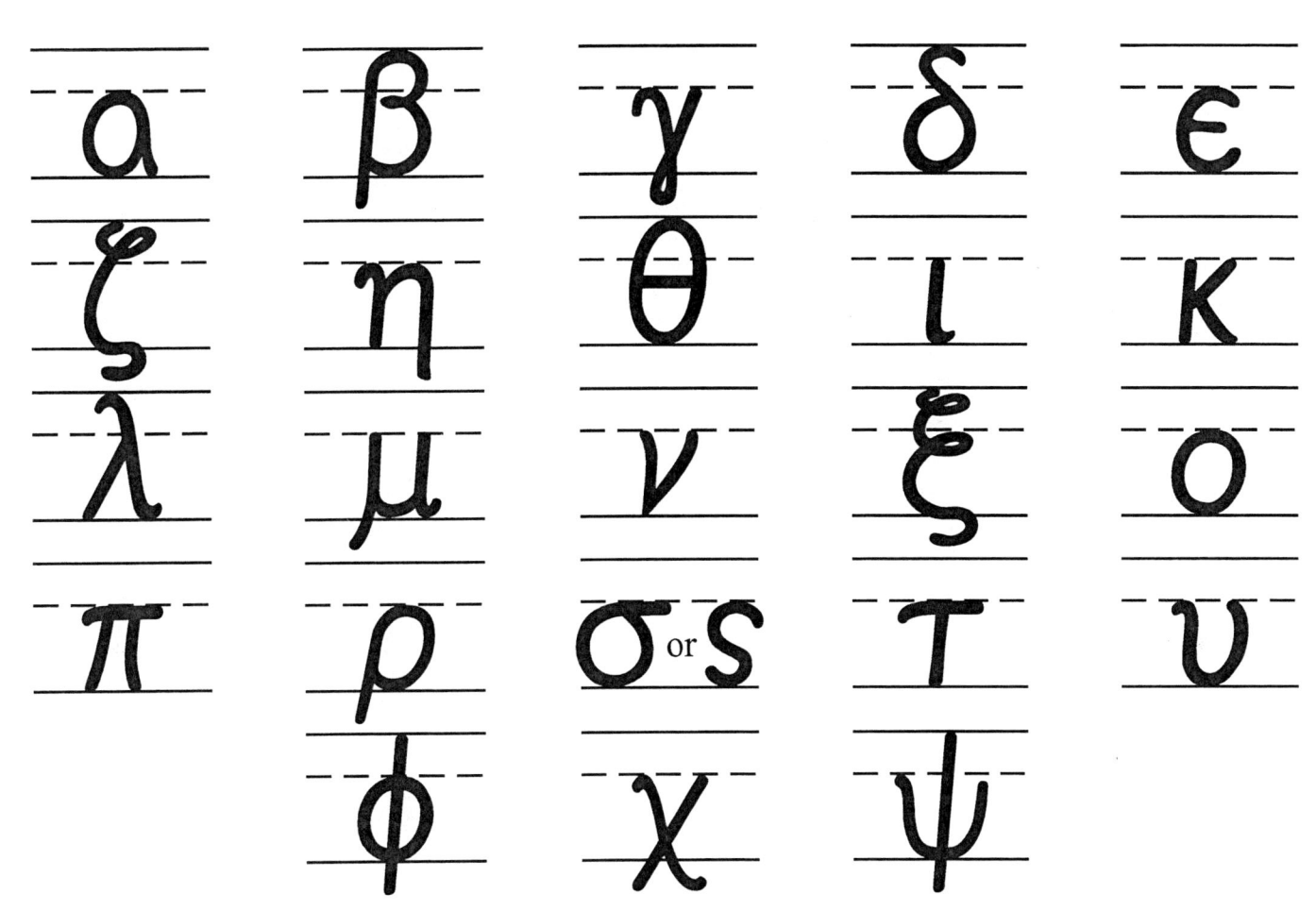

| α | β | γ | δ | ε |
| --- | --- | --- | --- | --- |
| ζ | η | θ | ι | κ |
| λ | μ | ν | ξ | ο |
| π | ρ | σ or ς | τ | υ |
|   | φ | χ | ψ |   |

Look at the circled letter in each box. Which Greek letter comes next? Circle it.

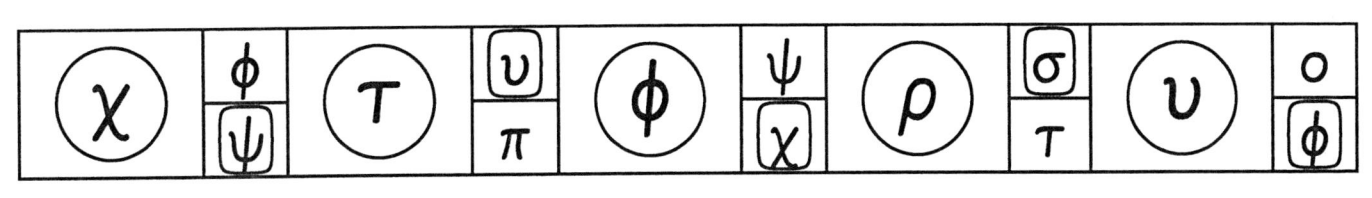

| ⓧ | φ / ψ̄ | ⓣ | ῡ / π | ⓕ | ψ̄ / χ | ⓡ | σ̄ / τ | ⓤ | ō / φ |

☐ I practiced my flashcards today.

# LET'S PRACTICE

Blast the rockets to their moons.

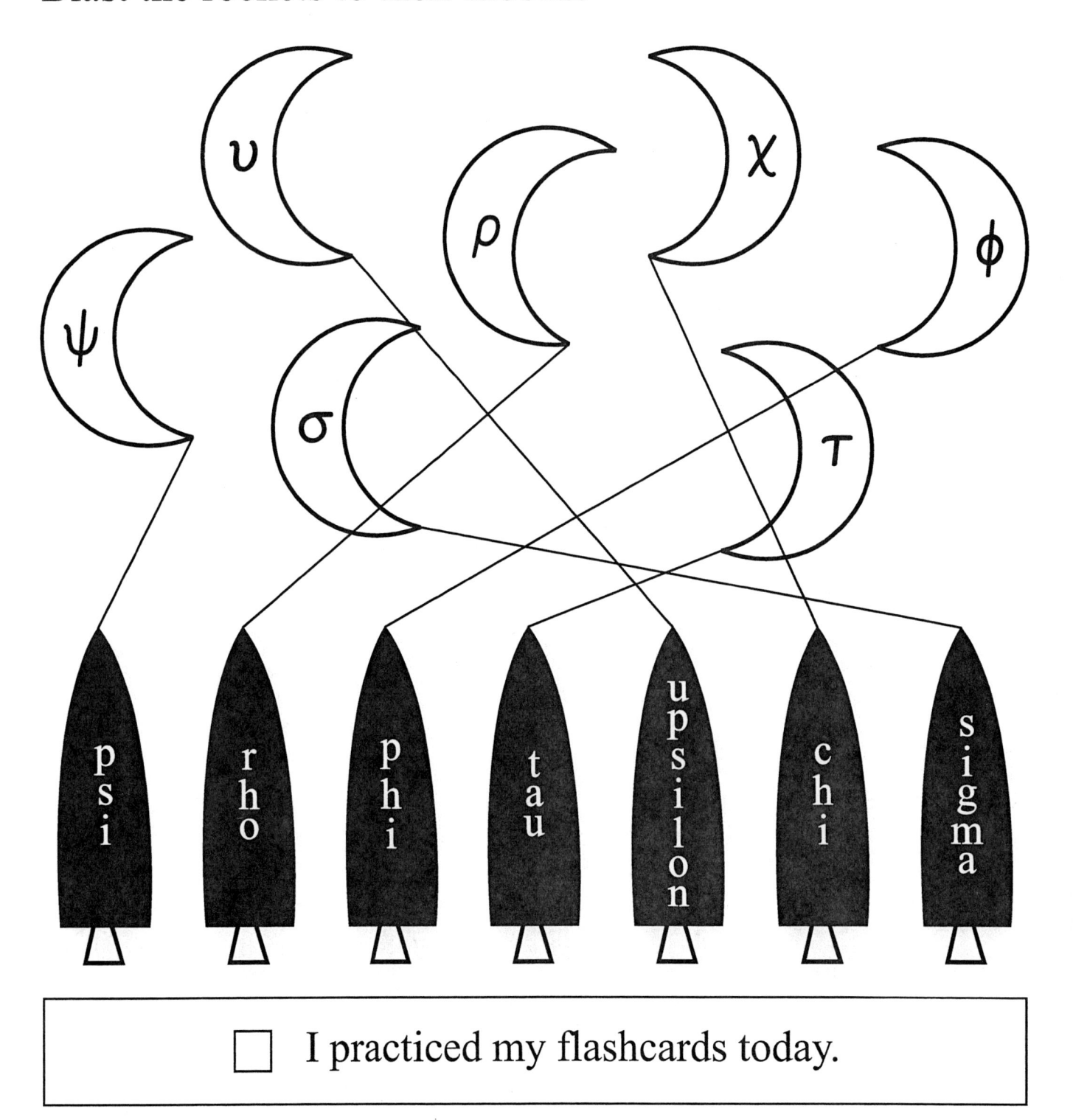

☐ I practiced my flashcards today.

Lesson 24

# OMEGA

Write the letter *omega* across each line.
As you write it, say "o-**may**-ga."

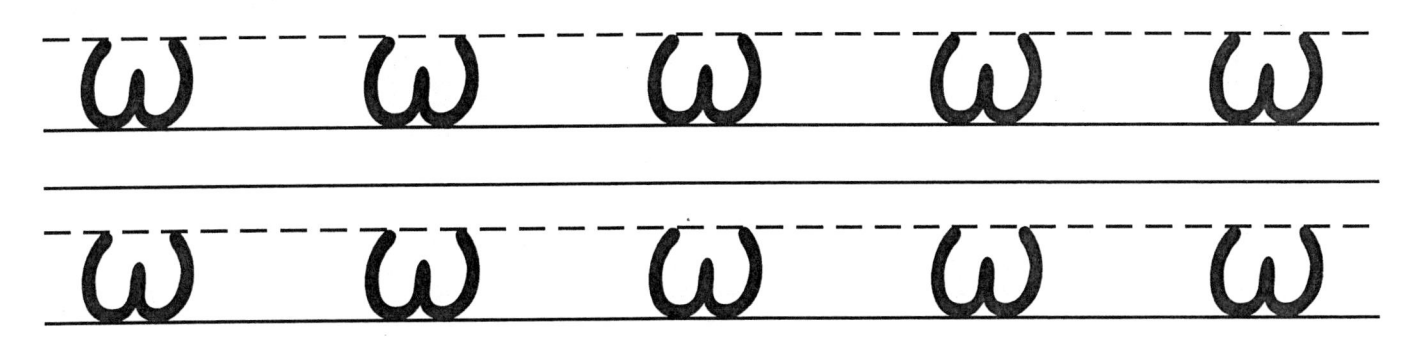

ω   ω   ω   ω   ω

ω   ω   ω   ω   ω

# More Practice with OMEGA

## Omega sounds like **o** in *note*.

ω ω ω ω ω

ω ω ω ω ω

ω ω ω ω ω

ω ω ω ω ω

ω ω ω ω ω

ω ω ω ω ω

☐ I practiced my flashcards today.
(Remember to add this new card to your flashcards.)

# LET'S PRACTICE

Write twenty-four letters of the Greek alphabet in order.

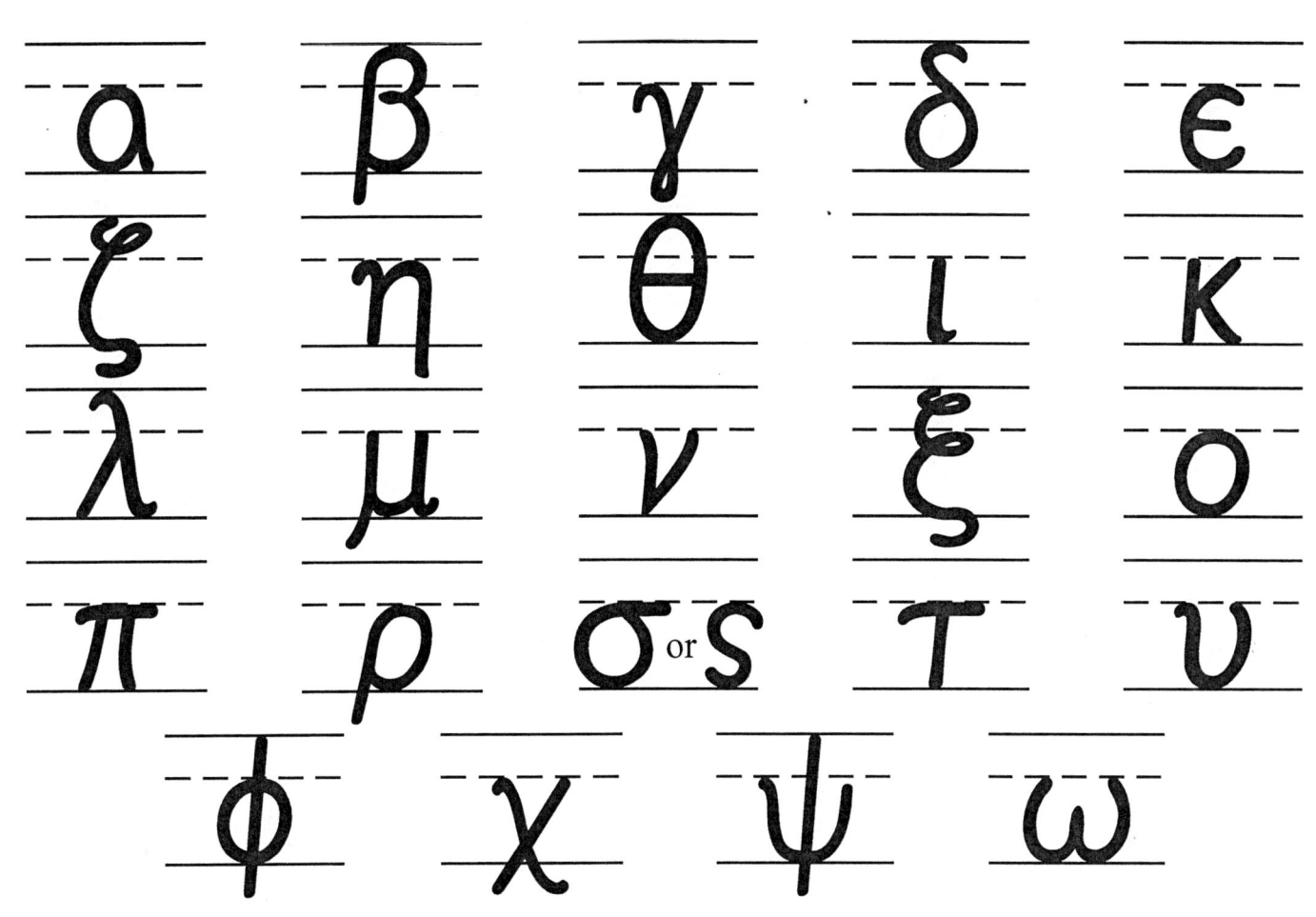

α  β  γ  δ  ε
ζ  η  θ  ι  κ
λ  μ  ν  ξ  ο
π  ρ  σ or ς  τ  υ
φ  χ  ψ  ω

Blacken the boxes with Greek letters to find a message.

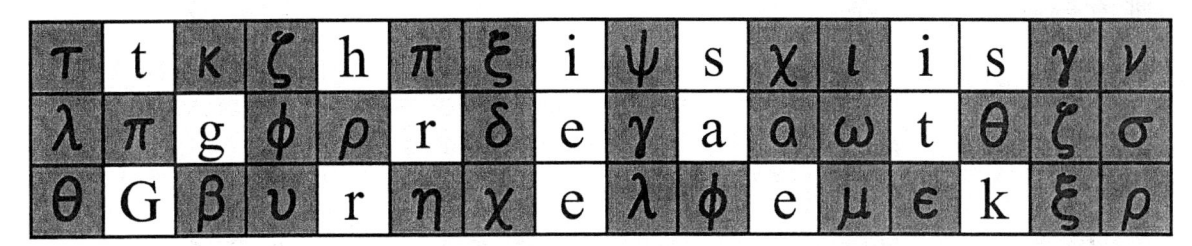

| τ | t | κ | ζ | h | π | ξ | i | ψ | s | χ | ι | i | s | γ | ν |
| λ | π | g | φ | ρ | r | δ | e | γ | a | α | ω | t | θ | ζ | σ |
| θ | G | β | υ | r | η | χ | e | λ | φ | e | μ | ε | k | ξ | ρ |

☐ I practiced my flashcards today.

# CHALLENGE!

Circle the names of the twenty-four Greek letters.

☐ I practiced my flashcards today.

Lesson 25

# κύριος

means

# Lord

It sounds like **koo**-ree-os.

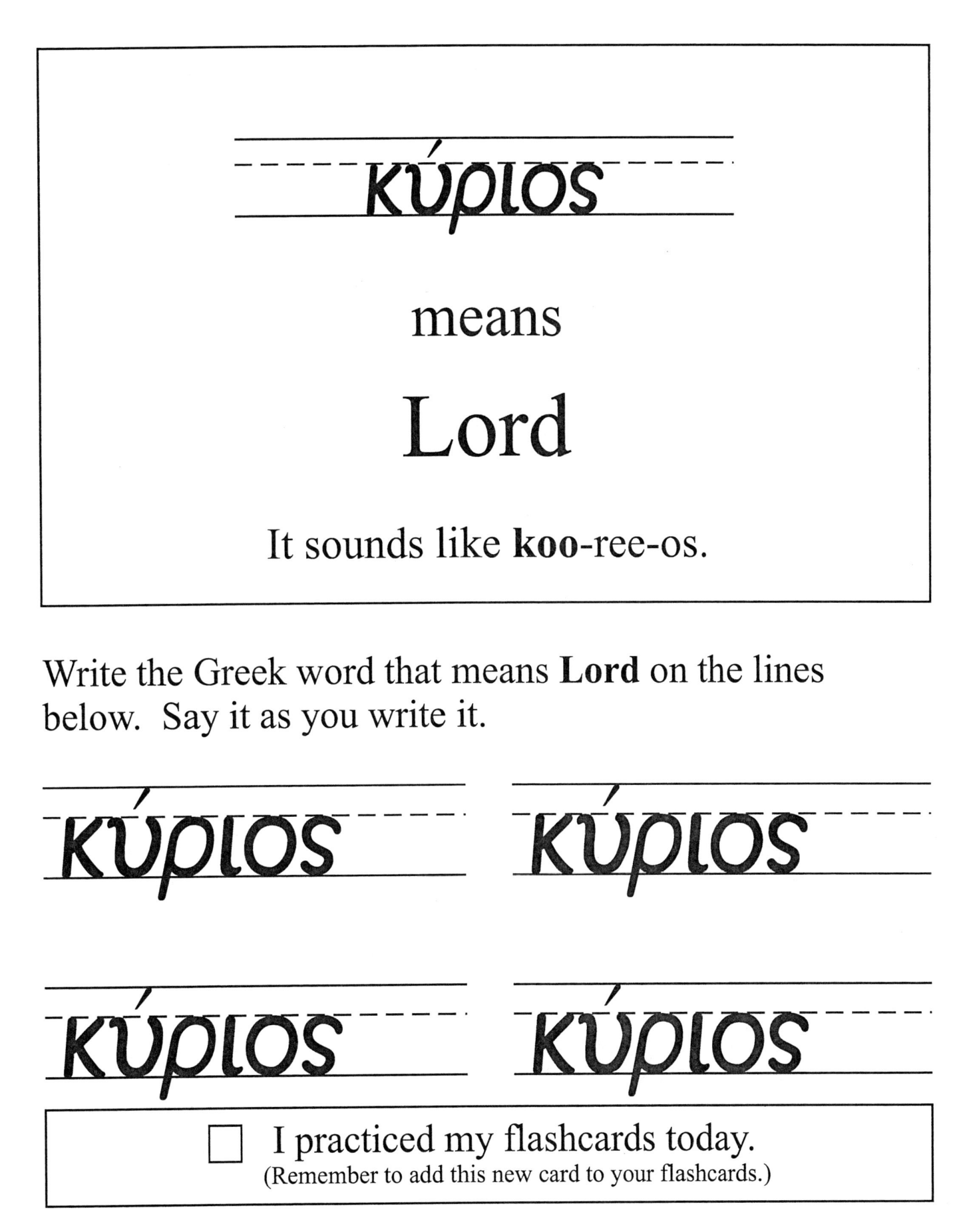

Write the Greek word that means **Lord** on the lines below. Say it as you write it.

κύριος         κύριος

κύριος         κύριος

☐ I practiced my flashcards today.
(Remember to add this new card to your flashcards.)

Greek Workbook - Level 1
Copyright © 1994 by Karen Mohs

# More Practice with κύριος

Write the Greek word for **Lord** on each fish.

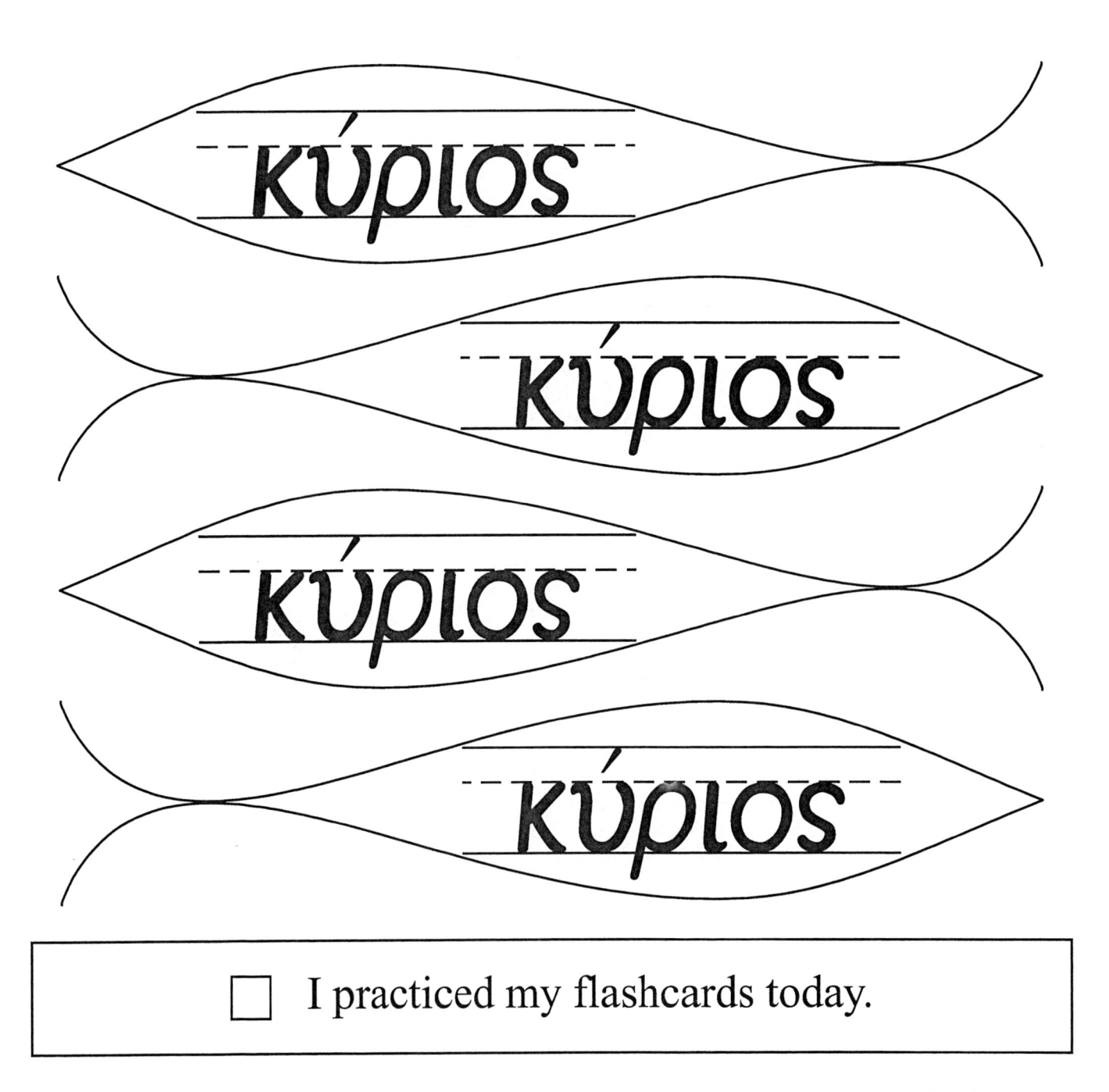

κύριος

κύριος

κύριος

κύριος

☐ I practiced my flashcards today.

Lesson 26

## ἐμοὶ

means

# my

It sounds like e-**moy**.

Write the Greek word that means **my** on the lines below. Say it as you write it.

ἐμοὶ  ἐμοὶ

ἐμοὶ  ἐμοὶ

☐ I practiced my flashcards today.
(Remember to add this new card to your flashcards.)

# More Practice with ἐμοὶ

Write the Greek word for **my** on each beach ball.

☐ I practiced my flashcards today.

# LET'S PRACTICE

Draw lines from the words to their meanings.

κύριος — my

ἐμοὶ — Lord

Write the meanings of these words.

κύριος   Lord

ἐμοὶ   my

Circle all the words that mean the same as the first word in each row.

| | | | |
|---|---|---|---|
| my | (ἐμοὶ) | (ἐμοὶ) | μύρον |
|  | βλέπω | μέλι | (ἐμοὶ) |
| Lord | κύων | (κύριος) | κλίνω |
|  | (κύριος) | κωφόν | (κύριος) |

☐ I practiced my flashcards today.

# LET'S PRACTICE

Put the apples on the correct tree.

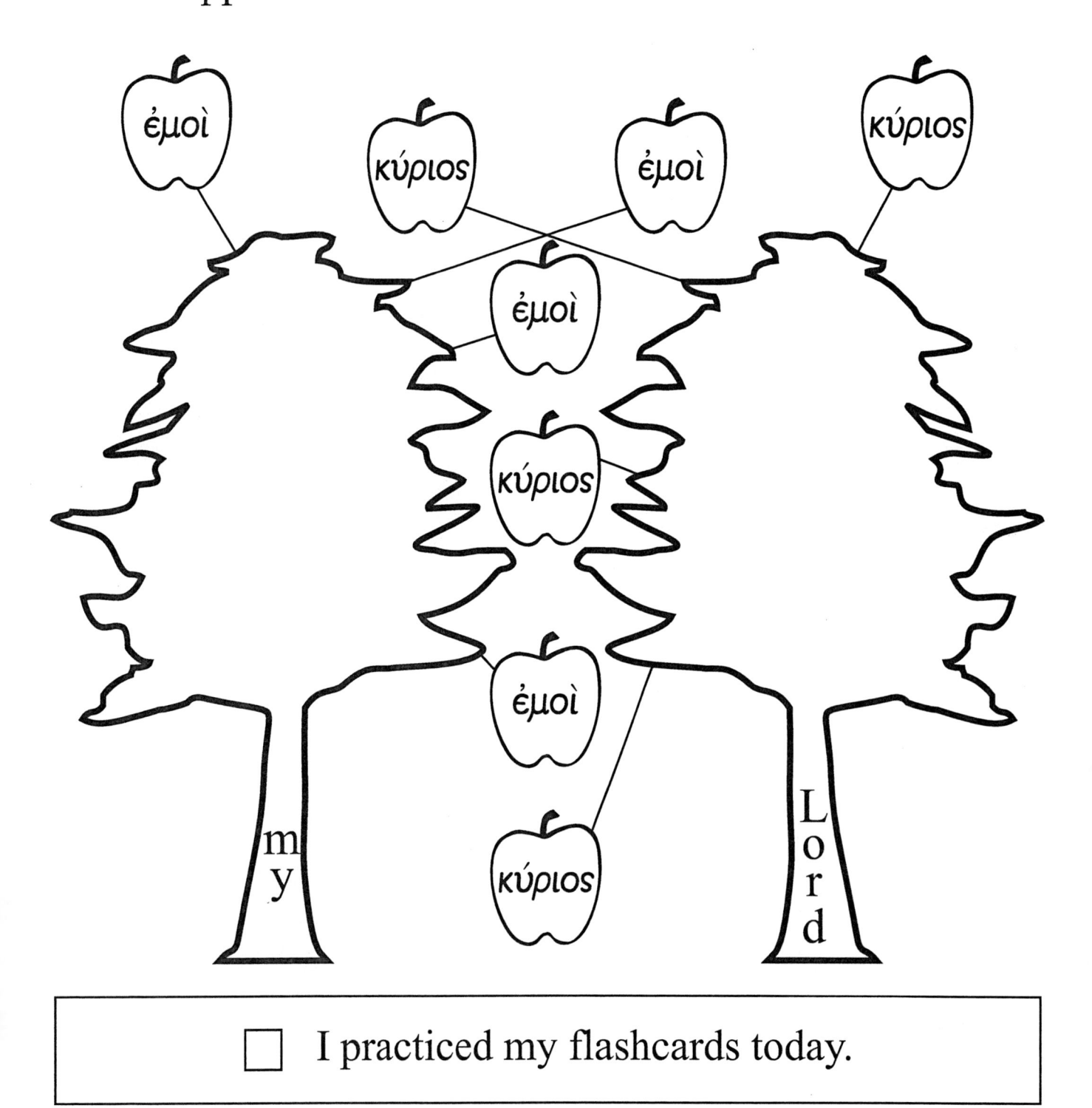

I practiced my flashcards today.

Lesson 27

## βοηθός

means

# helper

It sounds like bo-ay-**thos**.

Write the Greek word that means **helper** on the lines below. Say it as you write it.

βοηθός        βοηθός

βοηθός        βοηθός

☐ I practiced my flashcards today.
(Remember to add this new card to your flashcards.)

# More Practice with βοηθός

Write the Greek word for **helper** on each watermelon.

βοηθός

βοηθός

☐ I practiced my flashcards today.

# LET'S PRACTICE

Write the definition beneath each word.

| ἐμοὶ | βοηθός | κύριος |
|---|---|---|
| my | helper | Lord |

Circle all the words that mean the same as the first word in each row.

| | | | |
|---|---|---|---|
| βοηθός | (helper) | (helper) | doctor |
| | teacher | (helper) | teacher |
| κύριος | nurse | (Lord) | (Lord) |
| | cross | nurse | cross |
| ἐμοὶ | (my) | his | his |
| | (my) | your | (my) |

☐ I practiced my flashcards today.

Greek Workbook - Level 1
Copyright © 1994 by Karen Mohs

# LET'S PRACTICE

Draw lines from the balloons to the correct clown hats.

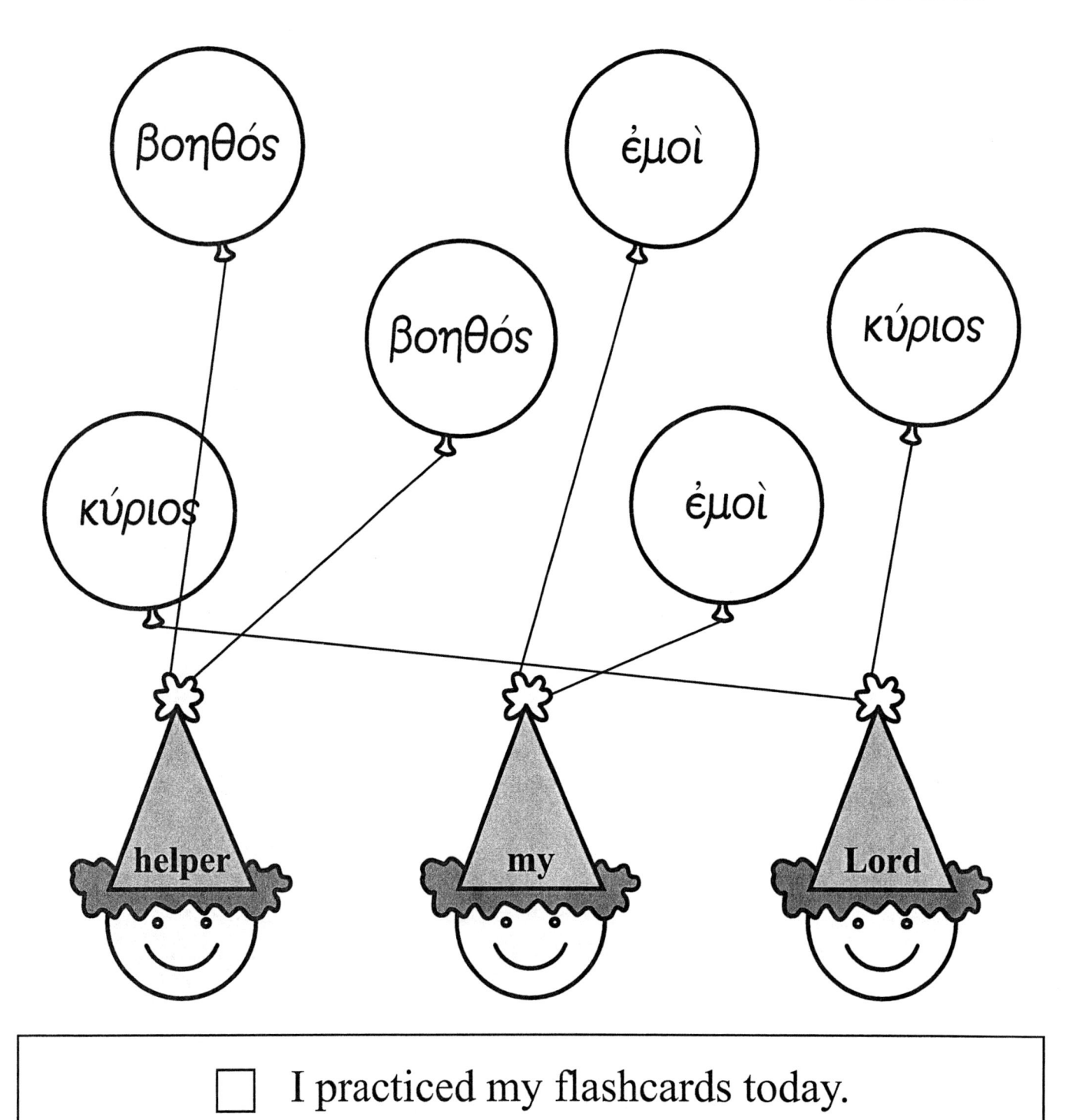

- βοηθός
- ἐμοὶ
- βοηθός
- κύριος
- κύριος
- ἐμοὶ

helper | my | Lord

☐ I practiced my flashcards today.

Lesson 28

# LET'S PRACTICE

Follow the trail. Each time you come to a Greek word you have learned, write it on the lines below.

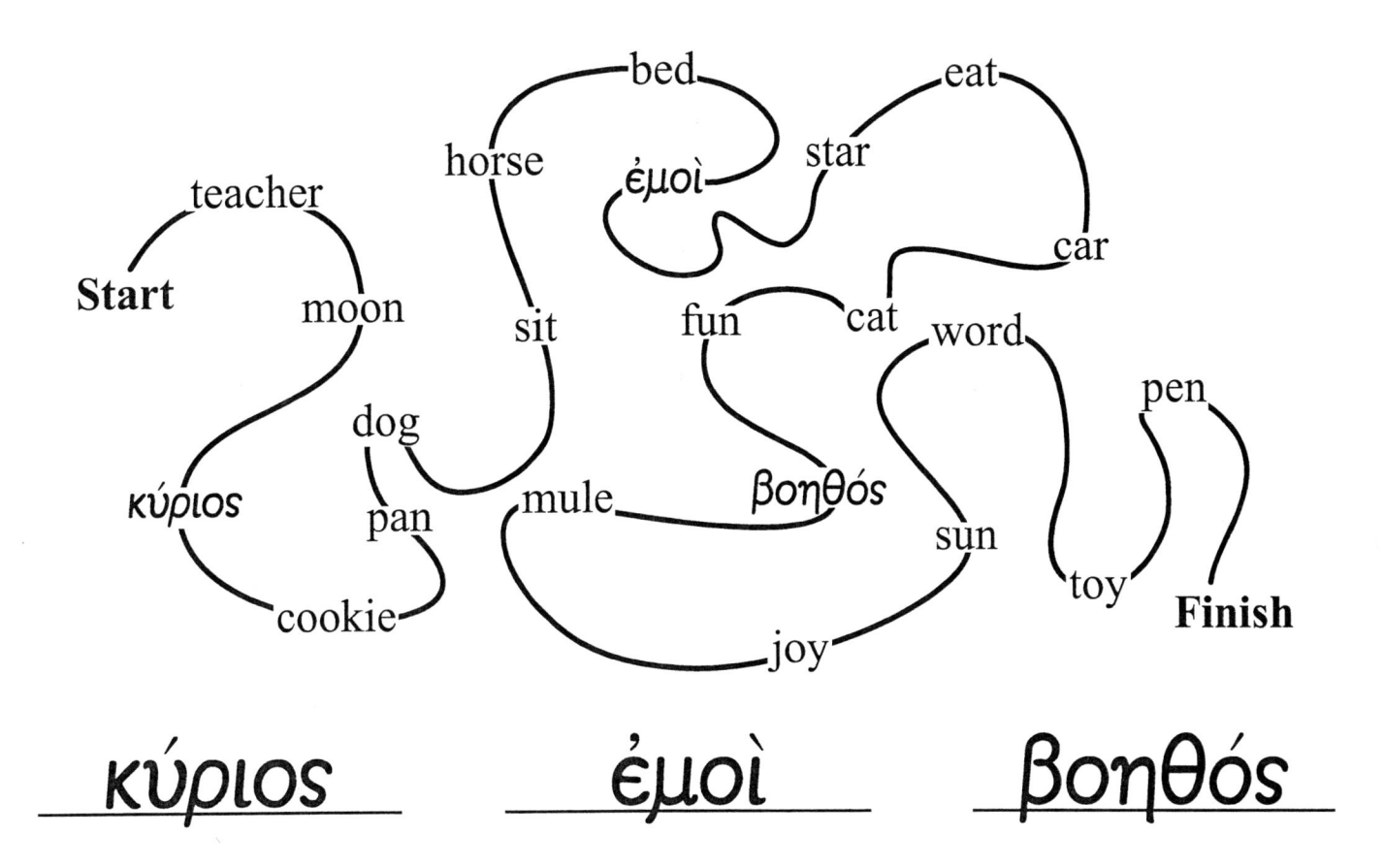

κύριος         ἐμοὶ         βοηθός

CONGRATULATIONS! You just wrote your first Greek sentence. Now see if you can write what it means.

The  Lord  is  my  helper .
(Hebrews 13:6)

☐ I practiced my flashcards today.

Greek Workbook - Level 1
Copyright © 1994 by Karen Mohs

# APPENDIX

## Greek - English Glossary

**α**
ἀγάπην - a love
ἄλλαι - others (women)
ἀνήρ - an adult man

**β**
βάτου - of a bath (liquid measure)
βιβλίον - a book
βίβλου - of a book
βλέπω - I see
βοηθός - a helper
βόσκω - I feed

**γ**
γέγοναν - they became
γίνομαι - I become
γογγύζω - I mutter
γραφή - a writing
γράφω - I write
γυνή - a married woman

**δ**
δέω - I bind
διδάσκω - I teach
δίδωμι - I give
διώκω - I pursue
δολόω - I bait

**ε**
ἐμοί - my
ἑτέρου - of another
εὑρέθη - he was found
ἔχω - I have

**ζ**
ζήλου - of a zeal
ζόφον - a thick darkness
ζώνη - a zone

**η**
ἥκω - I have arrived
ἠνοίγη - it was opened
ἤχθη - he was led

**θ**
θέσθε - (you) put
θηρίον - a wild animal
θύρα - a door, a gate

**ι**
ἰδίων - of one's own
ἰσχύν - a strength

**κ**
καθότι - according as
κέκληκε - he has called
κλίνω - I bow down
κόκκον - a kernel, a grain, a seed
κύριος - Lord
κύων - a dog
κωφόν - blunt, dull

**μ**
μέλι - honey
μύρον - an ointment

**π**
πέντε - five
πέπωκε - he has drunk
πέριξ - round about

**ρ**
ῥαντίζω - I sprinkle
ῥήγνυμι - I rend
ῥίπτω - I hurl, I throw, I cast

**σ**
σινδών - fine linen
σκηνήν - a tent
στάσιν - a standing or dignity

**τ**
ταῦτα - the same things
τίκτω - I bear
τρίτη - third

Greek Workbook - Level 1
Copyright © 1994 by Karen Mohs

109